Pocket Science

CHRIS OXLADE

AND

STEVE PARKER

mustard

This edition published by Mustard, 1999
Mustard is an imprint of Parragon

Parragon, Queen Street House
4 Queen Street
Bath, BA1 1HE, UK

© Copyright Parragon 1998

2 4 6 8 10 9 7 5 3 1

Produced by Miles Kelly Publishing Ltd
Unit 11, Bardfield Centre, Great Bardfield, Essex, CM7 4SL

British Library Cataloguing-in-Publication Data
A catalogue record for this book is available from the
British Library.

Editor: Steve Parker
Design: Geoff Sida, Angela Ashton, Sarah Ponder
Production Assistant: Ian Paulyn

ISBN 1-84164-029-8

Colour reproduction DPI Colour Limited
Printed in Italy

Contents

INTRODUCTION TO SCIENCE

A lmost everything you do depends on science. Whether you watch television, take a car ride, play computer games, go swimming or rollerblading, journey in a train or plane, have a bath or shower, munch a meal, ride a rollercoaster – science is involved, somewhere and somehow.

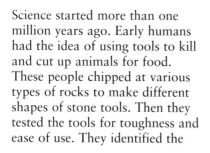

CAMERA

Science started more than one million years ago. Early humans had the idea of using tools to kill and cut up animals for food. These people chipped at various types of rocks to make different shapes of stone tools. Then they tested the tools for toughness and ease of use. They identified the best ones, carried out more tests, and improved them. These were the first scientific experiments.

The march of science

Scientific research has been going on ever since. Through the ages, people have invented and tested countless different tools, machines, processes and devices. Some, like the wheel, petrol engine and computer, have truly changed the world and the way we live. Others, such as the steam-car and mechanical calculator, came and went. They are now found only in museums.

Until this century, scientists and inventors mostly worked on their own. They tested and experimented in their lonely laboratories. They followed their own ideas and hunches, often working late into the night, using

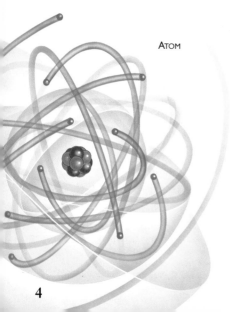

ATOM

simple chemicals and bits of string, metal and card. Some of them even died in explosions of their own making!

During this century, science has become big business. Huge numbers of people work in highly organized teams, using rare substances such as alloys and composites, and complex machines such as mass-spectrometers and 'atom-smasher' particle accelerators the size of small towns.

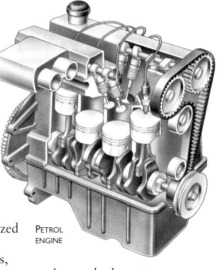

PETROL ENGINE

Science today

Our modern world is packed with the results of this scientific research and development. We have cars, planes, trains, ships, skyscrapers, bridges, tunnels, televisions, cameras, video recorders, compact disc players, radios, central heating, microwave ovens, fax machines, computers, the Internet … The list is almost endless, and growing day by day.

Science tomorrow

Scientific work has also given us greater understanding. We have knowledge about plants and animals, how they work inside, and how they survive in nature.

We can also look through huge telescopes into the depths of the Universe, and try to understand where stars came from, why they shine, and what might happen to them in millions of years. In the future, science will continue to make our lives more rewarding and enjoyable, and increase our knowledge and understanding.

DIFFERENT SCIENCES

▶ There are hundreds of different areas, or branches, of science – from astronomy to zoology. They are usually grouped into three overall categories.

▶ Physics looks at what things are. It studies what non-living substances are made of, from atoms and molecules, to planets, stars and galaxies.

▶ Chemistry looks at what things do. It studies how substances and materials join together, react or combine, to produce different substances and materials.

▶ Biology looks at living things. It is the study of plants, animals and other life-forms, and how they survive, feed, breed and adapt.

LIVING THINGS

There are millions of different animals and plants. They live all over the Earth's surface – from the icy Arctic and Antarctic to the dry, baking deserts near the Equator. They also live in the seas and oceans, from the shallow waters of warm tropical seas to the gloomy ocean depths. The study of living things is called biology. Biologists investigate how plants and animals feed, breed and survive.

Most of the living things we see are either plants (see page 8) or animals (see page 12). But many living things, such as mushrooms and germs, are neither plants nor animals. You can find out more about them on page 18.

Each animal or plant on Earth is an organism, and each different type of animal

or plant is called a species. All organisms try to grow and reproduce themselves so that their species continues to survive. They all collect substances, such as food, which they use to grow and live. They also make wastes, which are substances they do not need, and which are removed.

Plant or animal?

Plants get all the energy they need to live from sunlight. Animals get the energy they need to live by eating plants, animals or other organisms. Most animals can also move about, and they have

senses, such as sight, hearing and touch, which plants lack.

Building blocks of life

Most living things, including all plants and animals, are made up of incredibly tiny building blocks

△ **Evolution of life**
Living things have gradually changed, or evolved, over millions of years of Earth's history. The first life-forms appeared over 2,000 million years ago. Between about 200 and 65 million years ago, dinosaurs roamed the land.

called cells. Most cells are so small that you can only see them with a microscope. Some living things are just one cell. Others, such as oak trees, crocodiles and humans, are many billions.

THE FIVE KINGDOMS OF LIVING THINGS

———— MONERANS ————
Each is made of a single microscopic cell.
This does not have a nucleus (control centre) – unlike
all other living cells.
The group includes bacteria, viruses and similar 'germs', and
blue-green algae or cyanobacteria (which form 'scum' on ponds).

———— PROTISTS ————
Each is made of a single microscopic cell.
Each cell has a nucleus (control centre), unlike Monerans.
The group includes plant-like forms such as diatoms, animal-like
forms such as amoebas that can move about, and forms which
combine plant and animal features, such as paramecium.

———— PLANTS ————
Each is made of many microscopic cells.
Plants obtain energy from sunlight, by the process of
photosynthesis, and absorb raw materials from the surroundings.
Most cannot move around or react quickly to changes.
The group includes seaweeds (algae), mosses, ferns, grasses,
flowers, herbs, bushes and trees.

———— ANIMALS ————
Each is made of many microscopic cells.
Animals obtain energy and raw materials by consuming
(ingesting or eating) other living things or their products.
Most can move about, sense their surroundings and
react quickly to changes.
Includes sponges, jellyfish, corals, worms, insects, spiders,
crabs, starfish, snails, fish, frogs, reptiles, birds and mammals

———— FUNGI ————
Each is made of many microscopic cells.
Fungi obtain energy and raw materials by rotting or decay –
breaking down other organisms and absorbing the results.
Most cannot move around or react quickly to changes.
The group includes mushrooms, toadstools, yeasts, mildews,
blights and rusts.

PLANTS

Plants appeared on Earth millions of years before animals. They range in size from tiny mosses smaller than the dot on this i, through garden flowers such as roses, to trees nearly as tall as skyscrapers. Plants also live in the sea, from giant seaweeds to microscopic plant plankton.

Animals, including humans, could not live on Earth without plants. Most animals eat plants, or they eat animals which have eaten plants. Many animals use plants for shelter, nests and homes. We use plants as raw materials in hundreds of ways – buildings, bridges, furniture, cloth, paper and even medicines.

There are several different groups of plants. The largest is the flowering plants, which includes grasses, flowers, herbs and most trees. Non-flowering plants include conifer trees, ferns, mosses and the algae (which are mostly seaweeds).

Parts of a plant

A flowering plant has four main parts. These are the roots, stem, leaves and flowers.

Roots anchor the plant in the soil and take in water, minerals and nutrients. The stem supports the leaves and flowers. It also contains tiny tubes which carry water, nutrients, minerals and other substances around the plant. Leaves are shown opposite. You can find out more about flowers on pages 10-11.

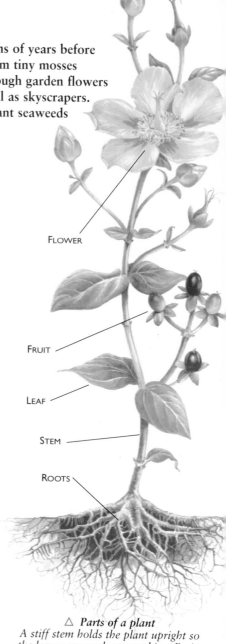

FLOWER

FRUIT

LEAF

STEM

ROOTS

△ *Parts of a plant*
A stiff stem holds the plant upright so the leaves can soak up sunshine. Fruits develop from flowers, and contain growing seeds.

How leaves make food

A plant's leaves capture some of the energy in sunlight. They use it to combine water, which is taken up from the soil, with the gas carbon dioxide, taken in from the air. The water and carbon dioxide join to make energy-rich sugars and other substances, which the plant needs to live and grow. This process is called photosynthesis.

▽ *Parts of a leaf*
A leaf is held out flat by a strong midrib with stiff veins branching from it. Veins are bundles of tiny tubes that carry nutrients and water.

MIDRIB

VEIN

BLADE

STALK

▽ *Woody plants*
A tree is a flowering plant with a very strong, rigid, wooden stem, called a trunk. This has layers or rings, each showing one year of growth.

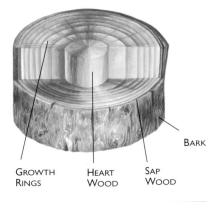

BARK

GROWTH RINGS

HEART WOOD

SAP WOOD

▽ *Inside a leaf*
This magnified view of a leaf blade shows the microscopic cells that capture sunlight energy. They do this with a green substance, chlorophyll.

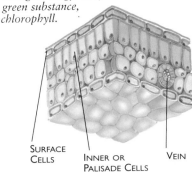

SURFACE CELLS

INNER OR PALISADE CELLS

VEIN

FACTS ABOUT PLANTS

▶ **Plant species**
Number of species (kinds) of plants: 375,000
Number of species of flowering plants: 250,000
Most ancient types of plants: Algae or seaweeds, which have been around for at least 1,000 million years
Most ancient type of flowering plant: Ginkgo or maidenhair trees, which have been around for 180 million years

▶ **Plant sizes**
Tallest: Coastal Redwood tree, California, USA (111 metres)
Largest: Giant Sequoia tree, California, USA (2,145 tonnes)
Largest flower: Rafflesia (90 centimetres across)
Largest leaves: Raffia palm (20 metres long)
Fastest growing: Bamboo (90 centimetres per day)

FLOWERS AND SEEDS

Plants do not grow flowers just to look pretty! Flowers are for reproduction – that is, making new plants. A typical flower has male parts and female parts. The male parts are the anthers, which produce pollen. The female parts are the stigma, which receives the pollen, and the ovary, which contains the egg cells.

Pollination happens when tiny grains of pollen from the anthers of one flower land on the stigma of another flower of the same kind (species). A tube grows from each pollen grain into the ovary. A microscopic male cell passes from the pollen grain along this tube to the female cell inside the egg, and joins with, or fertilizes, it.

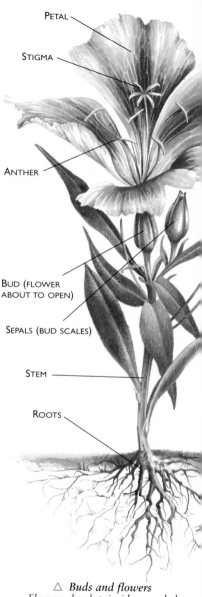

PETAL

STIGMA

ANTHER

BUD (FLOWER ABOUT TO OPEN)

SEPALS (BUD SCALES)

STEM

ROOTS

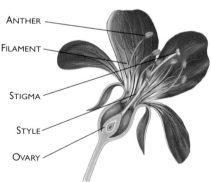

ANTHER

FILAMENT

STIGMA

STYLE

OVARY

△ *Inside a flower*
Pollen grains containing male cells develop inside anthers, which are on long stalks known as filaments. Female cells are protected inside the ovary.

△ *Buds and flowers*
Flowers develop inside rounded buds. Each bud grows on a stalk from the stem and is protected by greenish flaps called sepals. The bud opens or 'bursts' to reveal large, colourful parts known as petals.

Pollination and fertilization are necessary before the fertilized cells can develop into seeds.

Pollination

How do pollen grains get from one flower to another? In some plants, they are blown by the wind. In others, they are carried by small creatures such as insects, birds or bats. To attract these animals, the flowers have bright petals and strong scents. They also make a sugary liquid, nectar. As the animal sips the nectar, pollen grains brush onto its body. The animal then carries the grains to the next flower.

Fruits and seeds

After a flower is pollinated, it has done its job. The petals fall off and it seems to die. But inside, seeds are growing. The seeds are normally contained inside a fruit, which protects them. A plant tries to spread its seeds as far as possible, to give the seeds a good chance of growing into new plants. Many fruits, such as

▽ *Attracting insects*
Some flowers have dark lines on their petals. These are called nectar guides. Insects such as bees follow the lines, down to the nectary deep inside the flower.

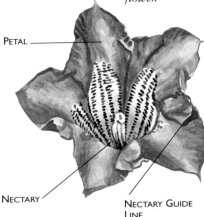

PETAL

NECTARY

NECTARY GUIDE LINE

berries, are very tasty, so that they are eaten by animals. The seeds inside the fruits pass through the animal's body and fall to the ground in its droppings, ready to grow.

Other seeds are light and fluffy, or have wing-like parts, and are spread by the wind.

◁ *Colour and shape*
Gardeners breed together different species and varieties of flowers, specially to produce varied petal colours and shapes. Breeding is done by collecting the pollen grains from one flower, often with a soft-bristled paintbrush, and stroking them onto another flower.

11

ANIMALS

Just as there are huge and tiny plants, there are huge and tiny animals. A blue whale is as large as a house, yet some insects are so small that they can be seen only with a microscope. Biologists guess that there are more than ten million kinds, or species, of animals on Earth. But millions of them have yet to be discovered.

Invertebrates

Animals are divided into two great groups, depending on what their bodies are like inside.

More than nine-tenths of animals belong to the group called invertebrates. Some have soft, jelly-like bodies, such as slugs, sea anemones and worms. Some have a hard outer shell to protect them, such as snails and mussels. Others have a hard outer

△ *The variety of invertebrates*
The scorpion belongs to the group of invertebrates called arthropods. These all have legs with moveable joints. Spiders, millipedes, centipedes and insects are also arthropods.

△ *In the water*
Fish make up the largest group of vertebrates, with more species than all of the other vertebrate groups combined.

△ *Crocodiles and other reptiles*
The main characteristics of the reptile group are a backbone (like other vertebrates), a covering of hard scales, four legs and a tail.

casing, or external skeleton, with jointed limbs, such as insects, spiders and crabs. Despite this variety, all invertebrates have one feature in common. They lack a backbone, or vertebral column, along the inside of the body.

Vertebrates

Animals with a backbone or vertebral column, and a strong skeleton inside (rather than outside) the body, are called vertebrates.

There are five main groups of vertebrates. The biggest is fish, which includes sharks, rays, goldfish, eels, pike and more than 20,000 other species.

The amphibians include frogs, toads, newts and salamanders. It is a much smaller group, with only about 4,000 species.

△ *Leaping amphibian*
Frogs and other amphibians have moist skin and most prefer damp conditions.

In the reptile group, which has about 6,200 species, there are lizards, snakes, turtles, tortoises, crocodiles and alligators.

Warm-blooded animals

Only two groups of animals are warm-blooded. One is birds, with more than 9,000 species. Their unique feature is feathers – no other animal has these. Birds vary from huge ostriches, eagles and hawks, penguins and owls, to tiny wrens and hummingbirds.

FACTS ABOUT ANIMALS
► **Animal species**
Total number of species (kinds) of animals: 10 million
Most common group: Insects, with at least 5 million species
► **Animal sizes**
Longest: Blue whale (more than 25 metres)
Heaviest: Blue whale (more than 120 tonnes)
Tallest: Giraffe (5.3 metres)
Fastest: Peregrine falcon (reaches 200 kilometres per hour in a swooping dive)
Fastest on land: Cheetah (sprints at 100 kilometres per hour)
Largest invertebrate: Giant squid (17 metres long)

Mammals

The other group of warm-blooded animals is mammals, with about 4,000 different kinds. They all have some kind of fur or hair, except for a few types of water mammals, such as whales, which are almost hairless.

▽ *Flying animals*
Only three groups of animals can fly in a controlled way, rather than simply glide. These are birds, bats and insects.

THE HUMAN BODY

A human body is far more complex than any machine, even a supercomputer. It is made of many different parts, called organs, such as the heart, brain and stomach. Each organ has its own special job to do, to keep the body alive and healthy.

Your body, like the bodies of animals, is made of billions of microscopic cells. There are many different kinds of cells, such as muscle cells, nerve cells, blood cells and skin cells. Each type of cell has a specialized shape, to do its job. For example, muscle cells are long and thin, but they can contract or shorten.

A group of the same cells makes up a tissue. For instance, a group of muscle cells makes up muscle tissue. This is found, not only in muscles themselves, but in other body parts, such as the heart, stomach, bladder and intestines.

An organ is made up of different tissues. For example, a muscle is mainly muscle tissue. But it also has nerves, blood and other tissues inside.

▽ *The body's skeleton*
The skeleton has 206 bones. In the head, the dome-shape skull protects the brain inside it. The ribs protect the heart and lungs inside the chest.

▽ **Muscles and movements**
There are about 640 muscles, ranging from the large and powerful gluteus in the upper leg, to tiny muscles in the face that make our facial expressions.

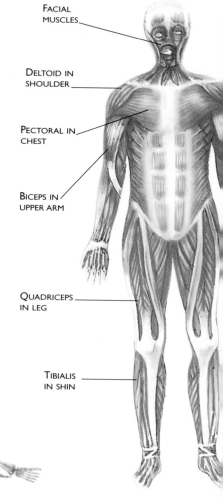

FACIAL MUSCLES

DELTOID IN SHOULDER

PECTORAL IN CHEST

BICEPS IN UPPER ARM

QUADRICEPS IN LEG

TIBIALIS IN SHIN

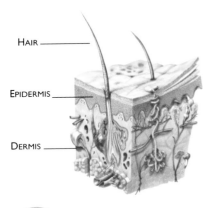

HAIR

EPIDERMIS

DERMIS

◁ **Magnified view of skin**
*Skin's outer layer, the epidermis, is dead
and tough. The lower layer, or dermis,
contains nerves and blood vessels.*

Each organ has one main job.
Your heart pumps blood. Your
blood vessels carry the blood
around your body. The blood
itself contains nutrients and other
vital substances that it delivers to
cells and tissues.

Body systems

A set of organs and tissues that
work together make up a body
system. The heart, blood vessels
and blood form the circulatory
system. Bones and joints form the
skeletal system, which provides
a strong supporting framework
inside the body. The muscles
make up the muscular system,
so that you can move about. The
mouth, gullet, stomach and
intestines form the digestive
system. The brain and nerves are
the nervous system, which
controls muscles and movements.

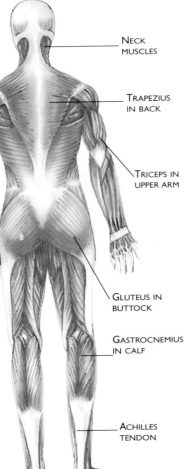

NECK
MUSCLES

TRAPEZIUS
IN BACK

TRICEPS IN
UPPER ARM

GLUTEUS IN
BUTTOCK

GASTROCNEMIUS
IN CALF

ACHILLES
TENDON

▽ **A scan of the brain**
*This medical CT scan shows the
wrinkled surface of the brain (grey)
inside the skull bone (white).*

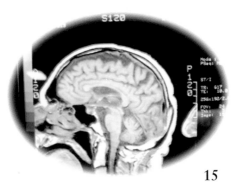

ANIMAL SENSES

We can tell what is happening in the world around us, using our senses. We have five main senses – sight, hearing, taste and smell and touch. So do many animals, from mice to moths. Each sense has its own sense organs, such as the eyes for sight, and the tongue for taste. Some senses are more complicated than they seem. Touch includes sensing physical contact, and also pressure, vibrations, cold, heat and pain.

Sense organs are specialized to detect something, such as light rays in sight, and turn them into tiny electrical signals called nerve impulses. These pass from the sense organ along nerves to the brain. The brain decodes and analyzes the signals, and then decides what to do. For example, if a dog steps on a thorn, it receives pain signals from its paw. So it moves its paw away quickly.

Useful senses

Each animal has an array of senses that help it to live, find food and avoid danger in its habitat. For example, an ocean fish has large eyes, to see through the gloomy water. A cave fish may have tiny eyes or none at all, because they are useless in its completely dark habitat.

Better senses

Many animals have senses similar to ours, but better. Horses can hear sounds which are so quiet that our ears do not detect them. Owls can see at night when, to us, it looks pitch black.

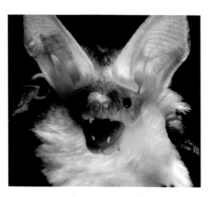

△ *Echo-detecting ears*
These huge ears hear echoes of the squeaks and clicks that the bat makes as it flies. The sounds bounce off objects, warning the bat that obstructions are nearby – even if it is too dark for the bat to see.

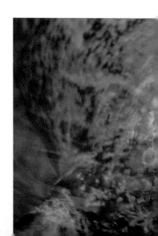

◁ *Senses at night*
A mouse has large eyes, to see even on very dark nights. It also feels its way with its long whiskers, and listens for sounds with its big ears. These are the senses typical of night-active, or nocturnal, creatures.

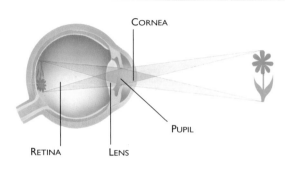

CORNEA

PUPIL

RETINA   LENS

△ *How an eye works*
Light rays shine through the clear front part of the eye, the cornea, and through a hole, the pupil. They are bent or focused by the lens, and shine onto the light-sensitive lining inside the eye, the retina. This turns the rays into nerve signals and sends them to the brain.

Extra senses

Some animals have senses that we lack. Most fish have a line of sensors along each side of the body, called a lateral line. This detects tiny changes in water pressure. It allows the fish to sense ripples caused by movements of other animals in the water, or by currents flowing past weeds, underwater rocks and other objects. Even in darkness, a fish can 'feel' its way using its lateral line sense.

△ *Making ultrasounds*
Dolphins, bats and other animals make very high-pitched sounds called ultrasound. Our ears cannot hear them, but the creatures themselves can. Dolphins use their ultrasound to find their way, like bats (opposite).

◁ *Feeling the way*
In dark, muddy water, a seal uses its long whiskers and eyebrows to feel its way. It can tell the difference between rocks, mud and food such as shellfish, simply by touch.

17

MORE LIVING THINGS

Mushrooms and toadstools might look like plants. But they are not plants. Or animals. They belong to a different main group, or kingdom, of living things – called fungi. There are also millions of microscopically small living things, such as bacteria and viruses, which are neither plants nor animals.

Some fungi are familiar to us in woods and gardens – and perhaps in the kitchen cupboard! They include mushrooms and toadstools, which grow mainly in shady, damp places. Bracket fungi grow like curved shelves from the trunks of old trees.

There are also other types of fungi. They include moulds that develop on old bread and other damp substances, the black slime that forms on rotting vegetables, and the rusts and mildews which attack crops such as wheat, corn and apples.

▽ **Microscopic skeletons**
Diatoms are protists (see page 7) that live in sea water. Each makes a rigid, see-through case for protection.

△ **Sprouting mushrooms**
Many types of mushrooms grow in soil or on old, rotten wood. They help the natural process of decay and recycling.

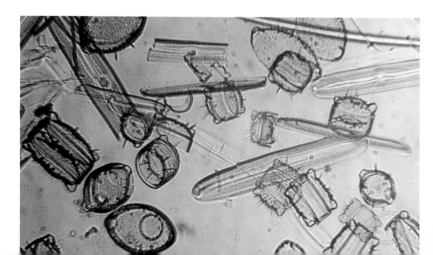

▷ *Making more mushrooms*
A young mushroom grows from the soil and opens its umbrella-like cap. From the underside of the cap, millions of spores are released into the air. Some mushrooms are edible. Others look very similar, yet they are deadly poisonous. It is essential to identify wild-picked mushrooms properly, before cooking and eating them.

A rotten life

Fungi normally live on the remains of dead plants and animals, such as rotting bodies, fruits, wood or food. They are vital to nature because they help to return nutrients, minerals and other substances to the soil.

Fungi are made up of a network of thin threads, mycelia. These spread into and through the rotting material they are feeding on. What we call mushrooms and toadstools are the reproductive parts, or fruiting bodies, of fungi. They produce millions of tiny spores, which look like tiny grains of dust. These float away in the air. If they settle in a suitable place, they begin to grow into new threads.

Bacteria

In a spoonful of soil, there are billions of tiny organisms called bacteria. Each one is a single cell. It is not plant or animal, but moneran (see page 7). These soil bacteria feed on dead plant and animal material. Like fungi, they help to break down and recycle minerals and nutrients.

Bacteria also live by their billions in your intestines, in your mouth and on your skin. They are nearly all harmless. But some, like salmonella, can be harmful. Other bacteria cause diseases such as meningitis, typhoid, cholera and gangrene.

◁ *Bacteria-made pills*
Some types of bacteria, such as certain kinds of Escherichia, have been genetically changed by bio-engineers. The bacteria are grown in huge vats and make useful products such as medicinal pills and drugs.

19

THE ENVIRONMENT

Where do you live? In a house, apartment or mansion? In a city, town or village? Are you surrounded by trees and fields, or buildings and roads? Is the weather usually warm or cold? All of these features make up your habitat – the surroundings you live in. All living things have their favourite habitats, too. The study of how organisms live in their habitat, finding food and shelter and mates, and surviving predators and dangers, is called ecology.

A habitat is where an animal or plant usually lives. For example, an earthworm's habitat is the soil. A cow's habitat is a grassy field. A crab's habitat is the seashore.

Plants and animals which live in a certain habitat have features to help them survive the conditions there. In the desert, a cactus has very long roots, to help it find water deep in the ground. In the ocean, fish have large tails for fast swimming, to help them catch prey or escape enemies. Features that help an organism to survive in its habitat are called adaptations. Some organisms live in several habitats. For example, foxes can survive in woods, scrubland, farmland and cities.

△ *Drawn by the need to drink*
All animals, plants and other living things need water to survive. In drought conditions, even predators and prey gather at waterholes.

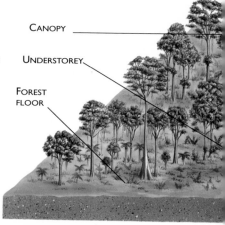

CANOPY

UNDERSTOREY

FOREST FLOOR

Ecosystems

An ecosystem is made up of a habitat and all the animals, plants and other organisms which live there. They are linked together by the way they feed.

In woodland, plants 'feed' on the minerals and nutrients in the soil. Caterpillars eat the leaves on plants. Small birds eat the caterpillars. Bigger birds such as hawks eat the small birds. These feeding links build up into a food web.

▽ *Cold conifer forests*
In the far north and south, summers are warm but short, and winters are long and icy. Conifer trees are adapted to these conditions. The needle-like leaves can withstand frost and stay on the trees all year.

EVERGREEN CONIFERS

DECIDUOUS TREES HAVE LEAVES ONLY IN SUMMER

◁ *Temperate woodlands*
In temperate lands, there are warm summers and cool winters. Trees sprout new leaves in spring, and many kinds of animals feed on them and produce young. In autumn (fall), trees lose their leaves and many animals hide away and sleep.

Habitat destruction

If a habitat is destroyed, the plants there die with it. The animals might try to escape. But they may well perish too, because they may end up in other types of habitats, where they are less well adapted. Every year hundreds of species of plants and animals die out completely, or become extinct, because their habitats are destroyed – usually by humans.

◁ *Tropical forests*
These habitats grow only in the warmest, dampest parts of the world. They teem with plant and animal life, such as giant trees, vines, creepers, monkeys and parrots. Because it is warm all year in the tropics, life thrives continually.

MATTER AND CHEMISTRY

Chemistry is the study of matter, substances and chemicals. It investigates what matter is made of and how substances combine or react. Using this knowledge, chemists can create new, useful substances and materials – from medicinal drugs, to stronger metals, to long-lasting plastics.

All matter is made from tiny particles called atoms. So far, scientists have discovered about 112 different types of atom. A substance made up of atoms which are all the same is called a chemical element (see page 114). For example, the gas oxygen is an element. So is the metal iron.

A substance made up of different types of atoms joined together is called a compound. For example, water is a compound of the elements oxygen and hydrogen.

The atoms of different elements can combine in so many different ways, to form many thousands of different compounds.

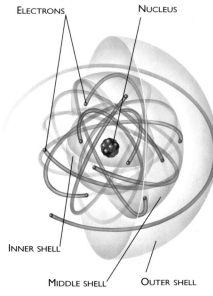

ELECTRONS NUCLEUS

INNER SHELL

MIDDLE SHELL OUTER SHELL

△ *Inside an atom*
All substances are made of atoms. An atom has a central part called a nucleus, with even smaller parts, electrons, whizzing around it.

◁ *A valuable mineral*
Ruby is a compound made from many different elements, including nitrogen, oxygen and silicon. These combine to form a beautiful, red, hard, glassy form of matter, called a crystal.

Molecules

When two or more atoms join together, or combine, they form a molecule. A molecule of the compound water has one atom of the element oxygen joined with two atoms of the element hydrogen. This can be written as the chemical formula H_2O.

Properties of matter

Scientists describe different substances in terms of their physical and chemical properties. At normal room temperature, substances like water are liquid, while oxygen is a gas, and iron is a solid (see page 24).

Other properties include heaviness or density, strength, the temperatures at which they melt (turn from solid to liquid) and boil (change from liquid to gas), how well they conduct electricity and heat, and so on.

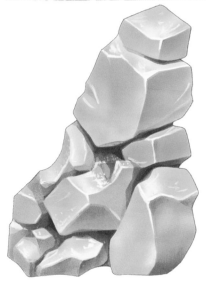

△ *A yellow element*
Sulphur is a chemical element. All of its atoms are exactly the same. When heated, powdery solid sulphur melts into a liquid at 113°C. Heated more, it boils into a gas at 445°C.

▽ *Substances that form crystals*
Many substances, from sugar and salt to diamond and ruby, are in the form of crystals. There are seven main types, or shapes, of crystals.

TRICLINIC

TETRAGONAL

MONOCLINIC

RHOMBOHEDRAL

CUBIC

HEXAGONAL/TRIGONAL

ORTHORHOMBIC

SOLIDS, LIQUIDS AND GASES

Imagine a glass half-full of water. This shows substances existing in the three different forms – solid, liquid and gas. These are called the three states of matter. The glass is a solid. The water in the glass is a liquid. The air above the water (and all around us) is a gas.

All substances are made from atoms, or atoms joined together into molecules. The way that these atoms and molecules can move about determine whether the substance is a gas, liquid or solid.

△ **See-through substances**
Some substances, such as water and glass, are see-through or transparent.

Gases

In a gas, the particles are widely spaced. They can also whizz about at high speed. This means a gas expands to fill the container it is in, because its particles are always free to move. If the container changes its size or shape, the gas does so too, and still fills the space available.

Liquids

In a liquid, the particles are packed closer together, but they can still move. A liquid flows so that it takes the shape of the container it is in. Gases and liquids are both known as fluids, because they can flow. But liquids cannot be squashed or compressed, unlike gases.

▷ **How particles move**
The state of a substance – gas, liquid or solid – depends on how its atoms or molecules can move about. In gases and liquids, the molecules can move about, which is why these states can flow.

GAS

PARTICLES MOVE FAST AND FREELY

LIQUID

PARTICLES MOVE MORE SLOWLY

24

Solids

In a solid, the particles are packed even closer together, and they are fixed so they cannot move. This means solids cannot flow. Most solids also have a fixed shape. They can be squashed, stretched and bent, but they return to their original shape when the forces are removed.

Changes of state

Most substances change from one state to another when they are heated or cooled. For example, when water is heated, it turns to gaseous water vapour (see page 42). When cooled, it becomes solid ice. These alterations are changes of state.

> **FACTS ABOUT CHANGING STATES**
>
> ▸ **Melting Points**
> The lightweight metal aluminium melts at 660°C.
>
> The common metal iron melts at 1,535°C.
>
> The metal titanium, used in jet engines, melts at 1,660°C.
>
> ▸ **Boiling Points**
> Aluminium boils at 2,467°C.
>
> Iron boils at 2,750°C.
>
> Titanium boils at 3,287°C.

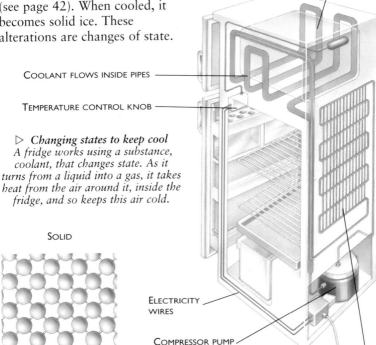

COOLANT ABSORBS WARMTH FROM AIR INSIDE FRIDGE

COOLANT FLOWS INSIDE PIPES

TEMPERATURE CONTROL KNOB

▷ *Changing states to keep cool*
A fridge works using a substance, coolant, that changes state. As it turns from a liquid into a gas, it takes heat from the air around it, inside the fridge, and so keeps this air cold.

SOLID

PARTICLES CANNOT MOVE

ELECTRICITY WIRES

COMPRESSOR PUMP

COOLANT GIVES OUT WARMTH TO AIR AROUND FRIDGE

CHEMICAL CHANGES

When ice melts to make water, the ice changes its physical form from solid to liquid. But it is still the same chemical substance – water, as molecules of H_2O. A chemical change is where a substance changes into another one which is chemically different, with molecules that have different atoms.

When a chemical change happens, a substance's molecules are altered. For example, if the gases hydrogen (H) and oxygen (O) are mixed at high temperature, the hydrogen and oxygen atoms join, or combine, to make water molecules (H_2O). This is called a chemical reaction

Some of the processes we see every day are chemical reactions. Burning things, cooking foods and rusting metals all involve chemical reactions. In the laboratory, chemical reactions are used to create new and useful substances from raw materials.

Breaking and making

The atoms in substances are joined together by links called bonds. When a chemical reaction happens, some of the bonds are

broken. The atoms become free. Then they join together in new, different combinations, to make molecules of the new substance.

There are various types of bonds, shown below. Some are harder to break than others. The usual way of breaking them is by increased temperature, or heating.

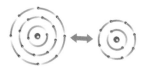

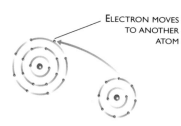

ELECTRON MOVES TO ANOTHER ATOM

△ *Ionic bond*
One atom loses an electron from its outer shell. The electron moves to the outer shell of the other atom, creating the link or bond.

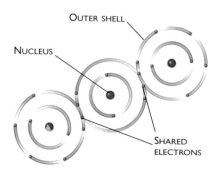

OUTER SHELL

NUCLEUS

SHARED ELECTRONS

◁ *Covalent bonds*
The outer shells of two atoms 'share' an electron between them. Sometimes the electron is more attached to one of the atoms. At other times it moves to the other atom.

▷ *A changing element*
Some elements can exist in different forms. An example is carbon. In nature it may be hard and shiny black lumps of coal, or a soft black powder known as graphite, or a hard and glistening diamond (see page 114).

Solutions

When you stir sugar into water, what happens to the sugar? It seems to disappear. Yet you can taste its sweetness in the drink.

The answer is that the sugar has broken up into its particles or molecules, which are too small to see, and which mix in among the water molecules. This is called dissolving. The water is known as the solvent. The substance which dissolves in it, in this case sugar, is the solute. The two together are known as a solution.

Water is an extremely good solvent. Many substances, from salt crystals to instant coffee granules, dissolve in it. Gases and liquids can also dissolve in water. In rivers, lakes and seas, creatures such as fish breathe by taking in the oxygen which is dissolved in the water.

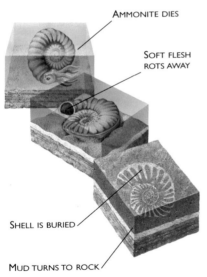

AMMONITE DIES

SOFT FLESH ROTS AWAY

SHELL IS BURIED

MUD TURNS TO ROCK

▷ *From shell to stone*
Fossilization is a chemical change that takes millions of years. The hard parts of a once-living thing, such as an animal's shell, tooth, claw or bone, are buried in mud. Gradually the part turns into solid rock.

SHAPE OF SHELL IS SOLID ROCK

27

MIXTURES

Many substances are mixtures of different substances. A mixture is not the same as a compound. Its particles are mixed together, rather than being chemically joined or bonded together. For example, stir sand grains into water, and you get a mixture of sand and water. You separate the parts of the mixture by pouring off the water. The parts are unaltered.

STALACTITE

There are many kinds of mixtures. A handful of mud is a mixture – of water, tiny grains of clay and sand, other soil particles, and other bits and pieces. A solute dissolved in a solvent, such as sugar in water, is another kind of mixture. So is a paste of peanut granules and peanut oil – as peanut butter.

It is often helpful to separate the parts, or constituents, of a mixture. This is done to obtain useful substances from the mixture, or to find out which constituents are in it. Three common methods of separating mixtures are filtering, distillation and chromatography.

STALAGMITE

▷ **Solids in liquids**
In a cave, water with lots of dissolved minerals drips from the roof and onto the floor. Over hundreds of years, tiny particles of minerals come out of solution and form stalagmites and stalactites.

Filtering
Filtering is used to separate a mixture of a liquid and a solid. The mixture flows through a filter medium, such as a sheet of filter paper (like blotting paper). The holes in the filter medium are big

◁ **Distilling a solution**
In the laboratory, a solution is heated. This turns the solvent into a gas, which floats away and is then cooled in the curly tube, back into a liquid.

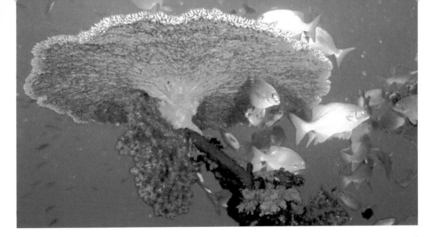

enough to let the particles of liquid to go through. But they are too small for the particles of solid. So the solid stays stuck on the filter paper, while the liquid drips through.

△ **Dissolved to un-dissolved**
In a coral reef, tiny creatures called polyps absorb dissolved minerals from sea water. They turn these into solid minerals, to make hard, stony cups around themselves, for protection. Millions of stony cups build up into the rock of the coral reef.

Distillation

If you had a mixture which is a solution of salt in water, how could you separate it? By distillation. This involves heating the solution. The water boils into water vapour, leaving the salt behind. The water vapour is collected and cooled back into liquid water. The salt gradually loses its water and becomes salt crystals.

Distillation is similar to evaporation. This means leaving a solution to dry out. The natural warmth of the surroundings makes the solvent turn into gas and float away, leaving behind the solute.

Chromatography

A mixture of a liquid and several different substances can be separated by chromatography. The mixture is passed through a chromatography medium. This is like a filter, but much thicker. The substances get trapped in different layers in the medium.

FACTS ABOUT SOLVENTS

▶ Chemical manufacturers use many kinds of solvents to make different products by distillation and similar processes.

▶ A useful but dangerous solvent is toluene (methylbenzene), which boils at 110°C

▶ Water is the most common and familiar solvent. It boils at 100°C.

▶ Another common solvent in chemical processes is alcohol (ethanol). It boils at 78.5°C.

▶ The solvent which gives nail varnish its characteristic smell is acetone (propanone). It boils at 56.5°C.

MATERIALS

Look around you. Start counting the number of different substances and materials you can see, which have been made into objects and items. There might be a metal chair, a plastic casing and pieces of paper. How about card, wood and cloth? Why is each material chosen for its specific job?

All the materials you can see began as natural substances. They came from the Earth, in various forms. Some may still be fairly natural, such as a wooden table. But other materials have been changed a great deal by chemical reactions, manufacturing processes and other treatments.

Metals

We use metals where we need a strong, hard, long-lasting material, or a material which conducts heat or electricity well. Iron is the most widely used metal. Most of it goes to make steel, which is used to make parts in many machines, from screwdrivers to cars, and in buildings. Another much-used metal is copper. It is a very good conductor of electricity and heat and is used to make electrical wires and cables, plumbing pipes and cooking pots. Drinks cans and kitchen foil are made from aluminium, which is light, strong and malleable – easily shaped.

◁ **Secret materials**
The Lockheed F-117 Nighthawk is a 'stealth' fighter plane. Its body is made of a special material designed to absorb or scatter the radio waves of radar. This means the plane is almost invisible on radar screens, and so less detectable by the enemy.

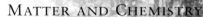

◁ **Designing new materials**
Chemists use computers to help them create new materials and substances. Molecules of the substance can be pictured on a computer screen, and changed in various ways, to give the material new properties. The substance is then actually made in the laboratory.

Materials from oil

Oil (petroleum), coal and gas formed deep in the rocks, over millions of years, from the long-dead remains of animals, plants and other organisms. They are called fossil fuels and contain complex mixtures and combinations of many useful substances. These are split up or separated at the oil refinery, mainly by the process of distillation (see page 28).

The results, known as petrochemicals, include fuels such as petrol, diesel and kerosene (jet fuel), and many kinds of oils, waxes and tars. These are processed further into hundreds of useful materials, from plastics and paints, to artificial fibres like nylon, polyester and acrylic. Our modern world depends greatly on materials made from fossil fuels. But at our present rate of use, these will last less than one hundred years into the future.

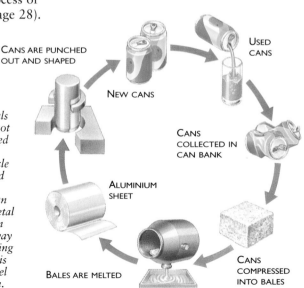

CANS ARE PUNCHED OUT AND SHAPED

USED CANS

NEW CANS

CANS COLLECTED IN CAN BANK

ALUMINIUM SHEET

CANS COMPRESSED INTO BALES

BALES ARE MELTED

▷ **Recycling**
The Earth's materials and resources will not last for ever. We need to use less raw materials, and recycle more manufactured goods. In some countries, more than nine-tenths of the metal aluminium, used in drinks cans, take-away meal trays and cooking foil, is recycled. This also helps to cut fuel costs and pollution.

31

AIR AND FLIGHT

Have you ever wondered why there is life on Earth but not on the other planets (as far as we know)? One of the main reasons is that the Earth is surrounded by a thick blanket of air, called the atmosphere. The atmosphere contains gases which plants and animals need to live. It also keeps the temperature on the Earth's surface steady. And it protects life from some of the harmful rays coming to Earth from the Sun.

The atmosphere gradually thins out as you go higher, away from Earth's surface. It eventually disappears completely about 1,000 kilometres up. Most of the air is far below this, in the lower layers. At the altitude of only 200 kilometres, the air is so thin that you would be in space. This is the height at which some spacecraft, such as the Space Shuttle, go around or orbit the Earth.

The air in the atmosphere presses equally in every direction on everything in it. This pressing force is called atmospheric or air pressure (see pages 34-35).

What is air?

Air is a mixture of around a dozen different gases. It is about four-fifths nitrogen and one fifth oxygen, with traces of other gases, mainly argon (see chart, right). There is normally some invisible water vapour in air, too, which makes it damp or humid.

Reactions with the air

Nitrogen, the main gas in air, is very unreactive. This means it does not react or combine chemically with many other substances. But the oxygen in air reacts with many substances. When things burn, they are combining with oxygen. Iron and steel also react with oxygen and water vapour in air, to make red-brown rust. This gradually eats away at iron-based metal objects.

◁ *Clear view through the atmosphere*
From the flight deck of a modern plane, you can see for many hundreds of kilometres. High in the sky, the air has fewer specks of dust and other floating particles, which tend to make the view hazy at lower levels.

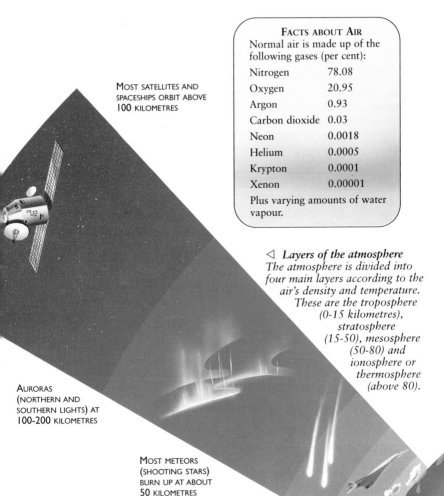

FACTS ABOUT AIR
Normal air is made up of the following gases (per cent):

Nitrogen	78.08
Oxygen	20.95
Argon	0.93
Carbon dioxide	0.03
Neon	0.0018
Helium	0.0005
Krypton	0.0001
Xenon	0.00001

Plus varying amounts of water vapour.

MOST SATELLITES AND SPACESHIPS ORBIT ABOVE 100 KILOMETRES

◁ *Layers of the atmosphere*
The atmosphere is divided into four main layers according to the air's density and temperature. These are the troposphere (0-15 kilometres), stratosphere (15-50), mesosphere (50-80) and ionosphere or thermosphere (above 80).

AURORAS (NORTHERN AND SOUTHERN LIGHTS) AT 100-200 KILOMETRES

MOST METEORS (SHOOTING STARS) BURN UP AT ABOUT 50 KILOMETRES

MOST CLOUDS AND WEATHER ARE BELOW 10 KILOMETRES

△ *The atmosphere*
The layer of air around the Earth gets thinner, or less dense, with height. More than three-quarters of the total weight of the atmosphere is in the 10 kilometres nearest the ground. It also gets colder with altitude. Average world temperature at sea level, or altitude zero, is 13-15°C. On top of the world's tallest peak, Mount Everest – almost nine kilometres high – the temperature is minus 50°C.

AIR PRESSURE

If you have ever used a bicycle pump, you will know that as you push the handle in, it seems to push back. This push is caused by air pressure inside the pump. The air pushes on the sides of the pump, too. In the same way, the air in the atmosphere presses on everything in the atmosphere. This is called atmospheric pressure.

Atmospheric pressure is caused by the Earth's gravity pulling the air downwards, towards the planet's surface. Because air is a fluid and flows, the atmosphere presses equally in all directions.

As you go up through the atmosphere, and the air gets thinner, atmospheric pressure gradually reduces. So does gravity. By about 200 kilometres of altitude, there is no air and things float about weightless.

Pneumatic machines

Air is used in devices called pneumatic machines, to transfer force or movement from one place to another, usually along pipes or tubes. Increasing the pressure at one end of the pipe, using a pump or compressor, makes the pressure rise all along the pipe. The pressure can be enough to make a pneumatic road drill smash concrete.

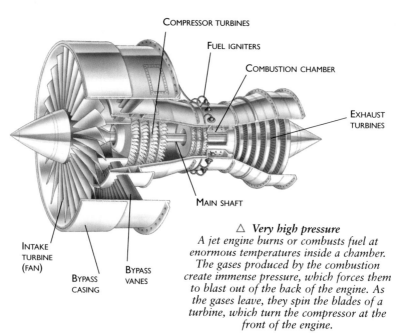

COMPRESSOR TURBINES

FUEL IGNITERS

COMBUSTION CHAMBER

EXHAUST TURBINES

MAIN SHAFT

INTAKE TURBINE (FAN)

BYPASS CASING

BYPASS VANES

△ *Very high pressure*
A jet engine burns or combusts fuel at enormous temperatures inside a chamber. The gases produced by the combustion create immense pressure, which forces them to blast out of the back of the engine. As the gases leave, they spin the blades of a turbine, which turn the compressor at the front of the engine.

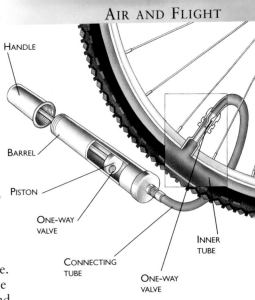

▷ Pressure and heat
Squeezing or compressing air into
a smaller space makes its
temperature rise. This is why a
bicycle pump gets hot as you use
it. The pump has a piston inside
which pushes the air in the pump
along the connecting tube into the
inner tube inside the tyre.

HANDLE

BARREL

PISTON

ONE-WAY
VALVE

CONNECTING
TUBE

ONE-WAY
VALVE

INNER
TUBE

Rising hot air

All gases, including those in air, expand (get bigger) when they get hotter. If a lump of air is warmed up, it expands to fill more space. This also makes it lighter and thinner, or less dense. So it floats upwards through the cooler, denser, heavier air around it. This area of moving air is called a convection current. You can find out more about convection currents on page 84 and about how they affect the weather on page 36.

Lighter-than-air flight

Lighter-than-air flying relies on the fact that hot air rises in cooler air. A hot-air balloon has a huge fabric bag called an envelope which is filled with air heated by the burner just below. The balloon floats upwards like a bubble of hot air, pulling the basket with it.

◁ A lot of hot air
A gas burner's flame fills the balloon's
envelope with very hot air, and so the
balloon rises. As the hot air gradually
cools, losing heat through the envelope
to the atmosphere around it, the
balloon begins to sink. So the hot air is
topped up regularly, by blasts of
roaring flame from the burner.

35

THE WEATHER

What's the weather like where you live today? Hot and dry? Wet and windy? Cold and still? All these types of weather happen because of air swirling about in the atmosphere, carrying various forms of water with it.

The weather happens in the lowest layers of the atmosphere. As the Earth spins and the Sun shines on rocks, forests, cities, lakes and seas, the Sun's warmth heats some parts of the surface and atmosphere more than others. The warmed air rises. This creates an area where the atmospheric pressure is lower than normal, which is called a 'low'. The space made by the rising air is filled by more air flowing from the side. As air cools and sinks, it creates an area where atmospheric pressure is higher than normal, known as a 'high'. Air flowing sideways is known as wind.

Clouds and rain

As warm air moves across the oceans, the Sun's warmth makes water evaporate from the surface. This forms water vapour which makes the air damp or humid.

▽ **Weather from space**
Photographs taken from spaceships and satellites show swirling patterns of clouds in the atmosphere. These signify high winds spiralling around a central area of low pressure.

△ **Measuring the weather**
A thermometer measures the temperature of the air. Warmth makes the liquid in the bulb expand, so it pushes further up the tiny tube.

If this warm air rises up into the atmosphere, for example, as it blows over a mountain, it becomes cooler. Some of the water vapour turns into tiny floating water droplets or ice crystals, which we see as clouds.

Eventually the liquid or frozen water falls back to Earth, as rain or snow. You can find out more about this movement of water on page 44.

Climate

Different parts of the world have different types of weather. The general pattern of weather in a place, over many years, is called its climate.

The climate depends on where a region is, on the Earth's surface, and how close it is to large-scale features such as oceans, lakes and mountains. Places near the Equator, around the middle of the Earth, have warm weather all year round. This is called a tropical climate. It may be dry most of the time, creating a desert. Or there may be a rainy season. A short but regular period of heavy rain is known as the

▽ *Limited by the weather*
Most modern planes have enclosed cabins to keep out the weather. In an open cockpit, pilot and passengers are buffeted by the wind and rain. This usually limits the use of such planes to fine weather.

monsoon season. Places farther away from the Equator have more marked seasons, including a warm summer and cool winter. This is a temperate climate.

The changing weather

The atmosphere traps heat from the Sun, keeping the Earth warm. This is the natural greenhouse effect. But certain gases, created when we burn fuels, are increasing the amounts of trapped heat. This is gradually making the atmosphere warmer. This 'global warming' may be changing the Earth's climates for ever.

FACTS ABOUT THE WEATHER

▶ The hottest recorded air temperature was 58°C in Libya, North Africa, in 1922.

▶ The coldest recorded air temperature was minus 89°C at Vostok Base, Antarctica, in 1983.

▶ The highest recorded wind speed was 371 kilometres per hour on Mount Washington, New Hampshire, USA, in 1934.

▶ The most recorded average hours of sunshine are at Yuma, Arizona, USA, with 4,055 per year.

POWERED FLIGHT

An aeroplane can only stay up in the air while it is moving forwards. This is because it depends on the flow of air over its wings, to provide the upwards force called lift.

▽ **Basic parts of a plane**
A modern jet passenger plane has more than three million different components, from large panels of metal to tiny microchips. Some of the main structural and control parts are shown below.

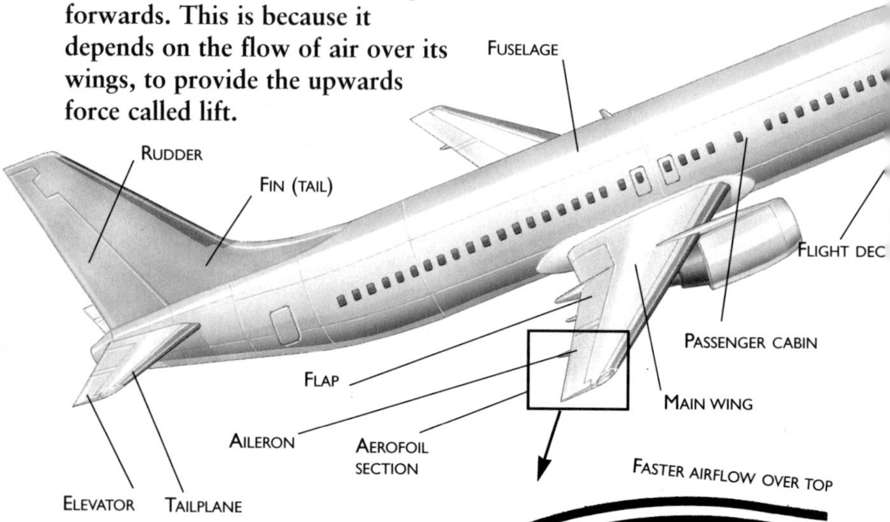

FUSELAGE

RUDDER

FIN (TAIL)

FLIGHT DEC

PASSENGER CABIN

FLAP

MAIN WING

AILERON

AEROFOIL SECTION

ELEVATOR   TAILPLANE

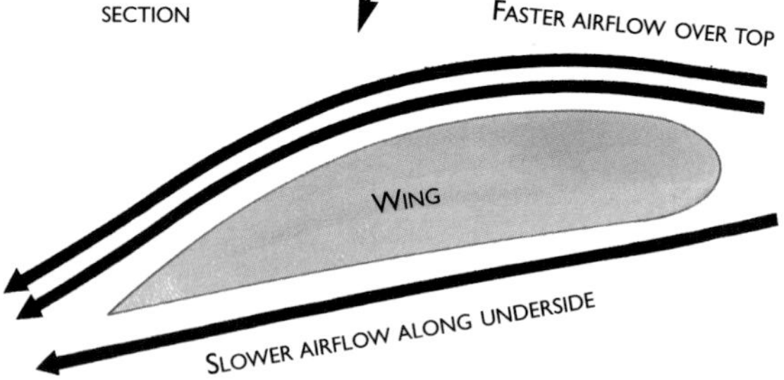

FASTER AIRFLOW OVER TOP

WING

SLOWER AIRFLOW ALONG UNDERSIDE

Wings make use of the fact that the faster air flows, the more its pressure drops. This is called the Bernoulli effect. If you could cut through a wing and look at the shape of the cut end, you would see a curved shape called the aerofoil section. When the wing is moving forwards through the air, air flows over and under the wing. The aerofoil shape makes the air passing over the top of the wing go faster than the air passing underneath the wing.

This makes the pressure above the wing less than the pressure below it. The result is a force called lift, that pushes the wing upwards. Rather, because of the lower-than-normal air pressure over the top, the wing is 'sucked' upwards.

Controlled flight

The horizontal wings provide lift to keep the plane in the air. At the back of most aircraft, there

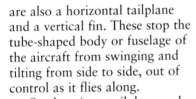

FACTS ABOUT FLYING

▶ **Fastest jet** The fastest jet-propelled aircraft is the Lockheed SR-71A Blackbird, a US 'reconnaissance' (spy) plane. It set the record for level powered flight in 1976, at 3,529 kilometres per hour (see page 41).

▶ **Fastest of all** The fastest aircraft of any kind was the Bell X-15. With tiny wings but a huge rocket engine, it reached 7,270 kilometres per hour in 1967.

▶ **In comparison** A normal passenger jet plane goes about 950-1,000 kilometres per hour. The Concorde airliner cruises at 2,150 kilometres per hour.

are also a horizontal tailplane and a vertical fin. These stop the tube-shaped body or fuselage of the aircraft from swinging and tilting from side to side, out of control as it flies along.

On the wings, tailplane and fin are hinged flaps. These are control surfaces. Those on the wings are called ailerons. They move up and down and make the plane tilt to the side, or roll. The hinged flaps on the tailplane are the elevators. They make the craft rise, or climb, and descend, or dive. On the fin is the rudder, which moves left and right to make the plane turn, or yaw, to the left or right.

Hovering flight

Some flying machines stay in the air without moving along. Helicopters have wings which spin and move through the air, rather than the air moving over them. They are long and thin, called rotor blades, and have an aerofoil section like an ordinary wing. They make lift even when the helicopter itself is stationary. This means the craft can hover – stay still in mid air.

▽ **Rotating wings**
A helicopter's main rotor blades are long, thin, twirling versions of a normal aircraft wing. The smaller rotors at the back counteract the natural tendency of the helicopter's body to spin in the opposite way to its main rotor blades.

AIR RESISTANCE

On a windy day, if you walk against the direction of the wind, you can feel it slowing you down. If you run, it slows you down even more. This is air resistance.

Any object that tries to move through air has to push it aside. The air pushes back, with a force called air resistance or drag. All fluids do this, including liquids such as water. You can feel the resistance of water when you try to run through it. Air is similar, but because it is a much thinner fluid, the resistance is much less.

△ *Faster than a bullet*
The latest 'bullet' trains actually go faster than a real bullet – more than 300 kilometres per hour. The air slips easily up the sloping front, with the windscreen at the same angle as the nose.

FACTS ABOUT FREE-FALLING

▶ A free-falling parachutist reaches maximum speed, or terminal velocity, less than ten seconds after leaping from the plane.

▶ The speed of free-fall can be controlled by the parachutist's body position.

▶ With arms and legs spread out to create maximum air resistance, the speed of free-fall is about 180 kilometres per hour.

▶ With arms and legs held close for minimum air resistance, the speed of free-fall is increased to about 250 kilometres per hour.

To overcome drag, the object needs a continuing push. This is called thrust. Trains, planes, cars and other vehicles have engines or motors. On your bicycle, it is your legs that do the pedalling and provide the thrust.

Terminal velocity

When you jump up, you come down with a thump. The higher you jump, the harder you land. This is because, as you fall, gravity makes you go faster and faster. When a free-fall

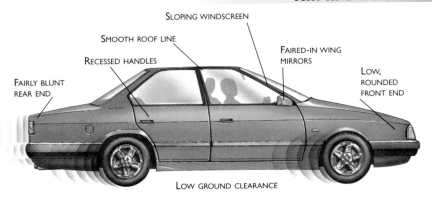

SLOPING WINDSCREEN

SMOOTH ROOF LINE

RECESSED HANDLES

FAIRED-IN WING MIRRORS

FAIRLY BLUNT REAR END

LOW, ROUNDED FRONT END

LOW GROUND CLEARANCE

parachutist jumps from a plane, he or she also goes faster and faster. But the drag builds up, too. Eventually, the force of the air resistance or drag pushing upwards becomes the same as the force of gravity pulling downwards. The parachutist does not speed up any more. He or she keeps going at the same speed. This maximum speed is called terminal velocity.

△ **Streamlining features**
A modern car has a smooth, rounded shape, with very few sticking-out parts. The bumpers, wing mirrors and similar parts are faired in, which means they are contained in smoothed-off casings that allow the air to slip past them very easily.

boxes. Drag is a nuisance for vehicles because it tries to slow them down, wasting fuel. This is why very fast vehicles such as aircraft and sports cars have such streamlined shapes.

Less drag

Smooth, streamlined shapes allow air to flow past them more easily. This creates much less drag than angular objects such as square

▷ **Ultimate streamlining**
The world's fastest jet plane, the Blackbird, is little more than a very long, slim, pointed fuselage and two huge engines on tiny wings. At Mach 3 (three times the speed of sound) even a tiny sticking-out surface can cause a huge amount of drag.

WATER AND LIQUIDS

How many liquids can you think of? How many of them contain water? Probably most of them. Only a few substances are in liquid form at normal temperature. Water is the most common of them, and it is a very special liquid.

Oceans full of water and dissolved salts cover two-thirds of the Earth's surface. There is fresh water in lakes and rivers. Water is also found in the atmosphere in the form of water vapour, and as ice at the Earth's poles and on mountain tops. And at any moment, on any day, there are at least a thousand rainstorms around the world.

◁ △ *Living in water*
Millions of animals, from sharks to jellyfish, and plants such as seaweeds, live in the salty water of seas and oceans. The salt water supports their bodies and buoys them up, but it is harder to move through than air.

Water is vital for life on Earth. All animals and plants need water to survive. Those that live on 'dry' land get their water from the soil or from streams, rivers, lakes, puddles, dew or raindrops.

Water is also vital for our own lives. We collect and store water for drinking and washing, for our pets and farm animals, and for irrigating crops. Each person needs to take in at least two litres of water daily, to stay alive and healthy.

States of water

Like many other substances, water can exist in three different states. Water is the liquid form. Ice is the solid form. Water vapour is the gaseous form (see page 24).

All of these forms occur naturally, with ice in cold places and invisible water vapour in hot places. Steam from a kettle is made up of tiny droplets of floating water vapour as it mixes with air.

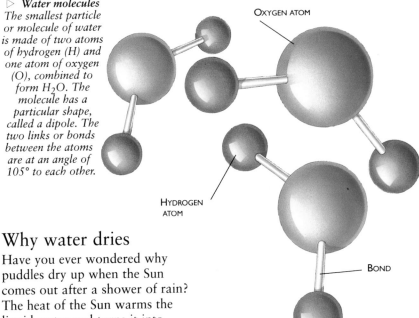

▷ **Water molecules**
The smallest particle or molecule of water is made of two atoms of hydrogen (H) and one atom of oxygen (O), combined to form H_2O. The molecule has a particular shape, called a dipole. The two links or bonds between the atoms are at an angle of 105° to each other.

OXYGEN ATOM

HYDROGEN ATOM

BOND

Why water dries

Have you ever wondered why puddles dry up when the Sun comes out after a shower of rain? The heat of the Sun warms the liquid water and turns it into invisible water vapour, which floats away into the air. This drying process is called evaporation. The hotter the Sun, the warmer the air becomes, and the faster evaporation happens.

The opposite occurs when you breathe on a cold mirror. Your breath is warm, coming out of your body. It is also nearly full, or saturated, with water vapour. The cooler air outside cannot hold so much water vapour, so the vapour turns back to water, as tiny droplets on the mirror. This is condensation.

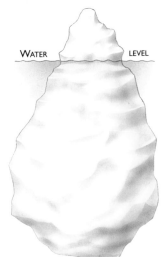

WATER LEVEL

▷ **Floating ice**
An iceberg is a huge lump of frozen water. About nine-tenths of its volume floats below the surface. Waves and currents wear it away, as it gradually melts.

43

WATER AND ICE

Water may seem to come and go, in many forms – as a flowing liquid, as tiny water droplets in clouds, as solid ice, hail and snow, and as invisible water vapour. But molecules of water are rarely made or destroyed. We see the same water, moving about and changing state.

▽ *Flowing ice*
In cold parts of the world, such as on high mountains, water is frozen into ice. But gravity pulls it, and makes it slide slowly downhill. This gradually flowing ribbon of ice is called a glacier.

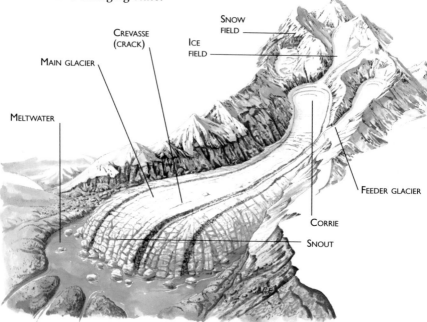

SNOW FIELD

CREVASSE (CRACK)

ICE FIELD

MAIN GLACIER

MELTWATER

FEEDER GLACIER

CORRIE

SNOUT

Water is constantly evaporating as water vapour into the atmosphere, from the world's lakes, rivers, seas and oceans. Water is also given off by plants, including the trees in forests and the crops on farmland. The warmer the water and the air, the more water vapour forms. Sometimes you can feel that the air has lots of water vapour in it..

We say that it is humid or 'sticky'. It often rains heavily or thunders in very humid conditions.

As air rises, it cools. The water vapour in it cools, too. It turns into tiny droplets of water or tiny ice crystals that we see as clouds. When the crystals or droplets get heavy enough, they fall from the sky as rain, or

44

◁ **Floating water**
Clouds are huge masses of billions of droplets of water. The droplets are so tiny that they float. Gradually they merge together, or coalesce, into larger drops. These are too heavy to float, and so fall as rain.

FACTS ABOUT WATER

▸ Freezing point of fresh water: 0°C

▸ Freezing point of sea water: minus 2°C

▸ Boiling point of fresh water: 100°C

▸ Density: 1 gram per cubic centimetre

▸ Area of oceans: 360 million square kilometres

▸ Weight of ocean water: 1.45 trillion tonnes

▸ Largest ocean: Pacific (166 million square kilometres)

▸ Percentage of Earth's fresh water in polar ice caps: 90%

sometimes as hail and snow. The general name for all these falling forms of water is precipitation.

Some of the rain that falls on the land evaporates again. Some is taken up by plants or thirsty animals. Some drains into streams and rivers, and eventually flows back into the sea. So water is always going round or circulating between the land, the lakes and rivers, the seas and oceans, and the atmosphere. This is called the water cycle.

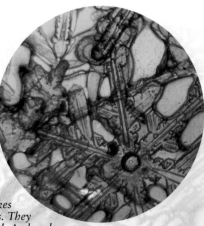

▷ **Frozen water**
Under the microscope, snowflakes have beautiful geometric patterns. They are always hexagonal, or six-sided. And each one is different.

45

WATER PRESSURE

Under the water, there is always water
pressure. It is caused by the weight of the
water above pressing down. But the water
presses in every direction, not just downwards.
Water pressure makes water flow along pipes
and out of the taps in your home.

LAMINAR
FLOW

FAST MOVEMENT
IN CENTRE

▷ *Flowing along a pipe*
Water does not flow smoothly in a
pipe. The regions of water next to
the pipe move more slowly, because
they rub against the pipe's inner
surface. The region of water in the
centre of the pipe flows faster. This
variation in speed of movement is
called laminar flow.

SLOW
MOVEMENT
NEAR EDGE

EDDIES
(SWIRLS)
AROUND
CORNER

In deep water, the
water
pressure gets
very high
indeed. If you tried to dive to
a depth of 100 metres, the
pressure on every square
centimetre of your skin (about
the area of
a fingernail)
would be
the same as
if a person was
standing on that
same area. So submarines need
very strong hulls, otherwise they
would be crushed by the pressure
under the sea.

Using water pressure

We use water pressure to make
water flow to, and around, our
homes and buildings. Is there a
tall water tower on a hill near

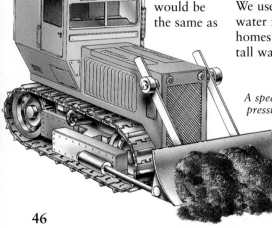

◁ *Hydraulic pressure*
A special type of oil, under very high
pressure, is used in machines such as
bulldozers and diggers. The
pressurized oil pushes on
pistons and levers, to make
different parts move with
immense power. Using
high-pressure liquids like
this is called
hydraulics.

your home? Water towers are high up so that there is plenty of pressure to push the water, through the pipes to your home, and out of your taps. Pumps are used to push the water from local reservoirs, lakes or rivers, up into water towers. In dry places, pumps are used to raise water from deep in the ground.

Surface tension

Water seems to have a stretchy, elastic 'skin' on its surface. This effect is caused by surface tension. It happens because the water molecules are attracted to each other, more than they are attracted to the molecules of air above them. Surface tension allows tiny insects to rest on the surface without falling through. It also pulls small blobs of water into rounded drops.

Capillary action

Look closely at the edge of the water's surface, in a glass of water. The liquid seems to 'creep' up the side of the glass slightly. This happens because water molecules are attracted to the glass, more than they are to each other. This pulls the molecules a small way up the glass surface. In a very narrow tube, this same effect pulls the water along the tube, even against the force of gravity. The effect is called capillary action. It makes water flow up the narrow tubes inside plant stems, from the plant's roots to its leaves and flowers.

▽ *How water cracks rocks*
Along coasts and shores, waves pound the land endlessly. Each big wave is like a high-pressure hammer blow. The power is enough to crack rocks and wear away cliffs.

FLOATING AND SINKING

Have you ever played with toys in the bath, to see which ones float and which ones sink? It might seem that heavy things sink, while light substances float. But if this is true, how can heavy metal ships, weighing thousands of tonnes, float?

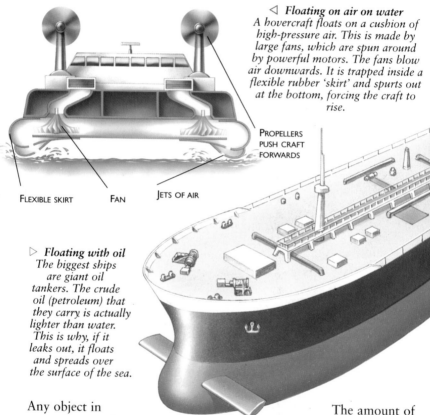

◁ *Floating on air on water*
A hovercraft floats on a cushion of high-pressure air. This is made by large fans, which are spun around by powerful motors. The fans blow air downwards. It is trapped inside a flexible rubber 'skirt' and spurts out at the bottom, forcing the craft to rise.

PROPELLERS
PUSH CRAFT
FORWARDS

FLEXIBLE SKIRT   FAN   JETS OF AIR

▷ *Floating with oil*
The biggest ships are giant oil tankers. The crude oil (petroleum) that they carry is actually lighter than water. This is why, if it leaks out, it floats and spreads over the surface of the sea.

Any object in water is pressed on by the water. This is water pressure (see page 46). The pressing is in all directions, including upwards. The up-push is called upthrust. If the upthrust on an object is greater than the object's weight, the object floats. If it is less, the object sinks.

The amount of upthrust on an object depends on how much water the object pushes aside as it dips into the water. Imagine a housebrick and a piece of foamed-plastic which is the same size and shape. If you lowered them both into the water, the foamed-plastic brick would float easily. It only needs

48

to push a small amount of water aside before the upthrust from the water is equal to its very light weight. The brick continues to dip into the water. When it is completely underwater, it pushes more water aside than the foamed-plastic

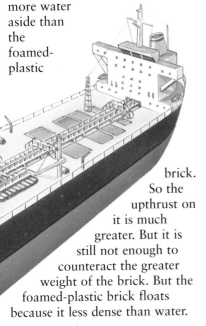

brick. So the upthrust on it is much greater. But it is still not enough to counteract the greater weight of the brick. But the foamed-plastic brick floats because it less dense than water.

Ship shapes

Most ships are made of metal. Metal is heavier than water, and a solid block of metal sinks. But a hollow block of metal floats because it is full of air. Adding together the air and metal, for the overall size of the hollow block, gives a density which is lower than the density of water. This is how metal ships float easily. Wooden ships float even better. If a metal ship has a hole, water leaks in and pushes out the air. As the ship fills up, it sinks. But a wooden boat with a hole would not sink, because the wood itself is less dense than water.

Diving and surfacing

Submarines are ships which can float or sink. Inside, they have ballast tanks. When the tanks are full of water, the submarine is heavy enough to sink. When air is pumped into the tanks, it forces out the water. As the tanks fill up with air, the submarine becomes light enough to float.

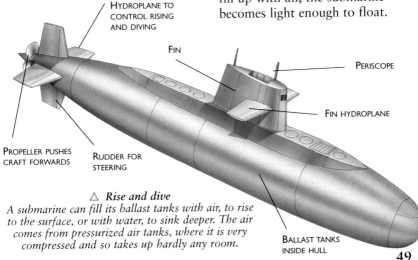

HYDROPLANE TO CONTROL RISING AND DIVING

FIN

PERISCOPE

FIN HYDROPLANE

PROPELLER PUSHES CRAFT FORWARDS

RUDDER FOR STEERING

BALLAST TANKS INSIDE HULL

△ *Rise and dive*
A submarine can fill its ballast tanks with air, to rise to the surface, or with water, to sink deeper. The air comes from pressurized air tanks, where it is very compressed and so takes up hardly any room.

49

WATER AND ENERGY

Huge amounts of water are always on the move. The water cycle causes water to flow down rivers. The gravity of the Moon and Sun causes water to ebb and flow in oceans, making tides. Winds blowing across wide expanses of water cause waves on the surface. All these movements have energy in them which could be captured and put to good use.

The simplest way of using the energy in flowing water is the water wheel. It is partly dipped into the water of a stream or river, and the flow of the water makes the wheel turn.

Water wheels are used in mills for working grindstones and other machinery. The river may

△ *Using wave power*
Sea creatures such as penguins use wave movements to help them, rather than fighting against the waves. They duck under incoming waves as they swim out to sea, to avoid being pushed back by them. And they 'surf' on waves as they return back to the land, thereby saving energy.

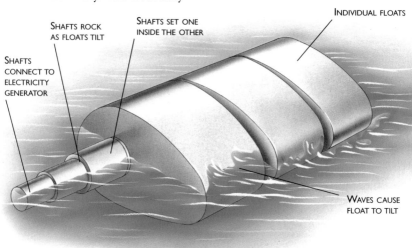

SHAFTS ROCK AS FLOATS TILT

SHAFTS SET ONE INSIDE THE OTHER

INDIVIDUAL FLOATS

SHAFTS CONNECT TO ELECTRICITY GENERATOR

WAVES CAUSE FLOAT TO TILT

▷ *Flowing energy*
Rushing water represents energy. This can be used to generate electricity. But not all fast-flowing rivers and spectacular waterfalls are suitable for this purpose. Some rivers are too steep and fast-flowing for the machinery to cope. Others vary too much in their flow rate, and may even dry up at certain times of year.

be channelled along a narrow specially-made course, to make its flow more powerful and faster.

Flowing water is used to turn generators (see page 78) to make electricity. The water flows through a turbine, which has fan-shaped blades, and makes the turbine spin. The turbine is linked to the generator. Electricity made in this way is called hydroelectricity (see page 94).

To make the flow of water more powerful and reliable, a dam is usually built across the river. The turbines and generating equipment are inside the dam. The deeper the water behind the dam, the greater its pressure, and so more electricity can be made. In some countries, such as Norway, hydroelectricity provides more than nine-tenths of all the electricity used.

◁ *Capturing wave energy*
There are many types of machinery designed to capture the energy of waves, so that it can be converted into electricity and used by people. This is the 'nodding duck' design. But waves vary in energy and direction, and cause damage if they are too powerful.

Hydro-problems

Damming large rivers for hydro electric power can create problems. Huge reservoirs upstream of the dam may drown wildlife areas and flood villages. Downstream, the water does not flow naturally, which can cause the river to clog up with mud or silt, or make the land along its banks less fertile.

SOUND AND WAVES

Think of all the sounds you hear in a typical day. There are probably dozens – friends and family talking, vehicles going past, birds singing, dogs barking, the wind blowing, aircraft flying overhead, music from radios, chat from the television, and all sorts of bangs and crashes. What makes all these sounds happen? Why are they so different? And how do you hear them?

Sounds are caused by things moving to and fro very quickly, which is called vibrating. Whenever something vibrates, it makes the air around it vibrate too. The vibrations spread through the air, moving away from the vibrating object. You hear sound because your ears detect these airborne vibrations when they reach you. If you touch your neck, you can feel your larynx (voice-box) vibrating as you speak.

Waves of pressure

The tiny vibrations that produce sounds are usually too small to see. They travel through the air as high and low regions of air pressure (see page 54). You can imagine these high and low regions as up-and-down waves, like the ripples on a pond. This is why we call them sound waves.

Sounds are a form of energy, like light, heat and movement. Sound waves are invisible because they are made by the movements of the atoms and molecules which

INCREASED AMPLITUDE

▽ **Moving as waves**
Light, sound and many other forms of energy travel as waves. The distance from a point on one wave to the same point on the next wave – such as from peak to peak – is called the wavelength. The amplitude is the distance from the middle of the wave to one of the peaks or troughs.

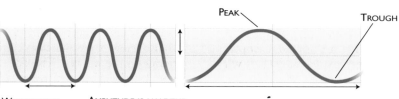

PEAK

TROUGH

WAVELENGTH   AMPLITUDE IS HALF THE WAVE'S TOTAL HEIGHT   INCREASED WAVELENGTH

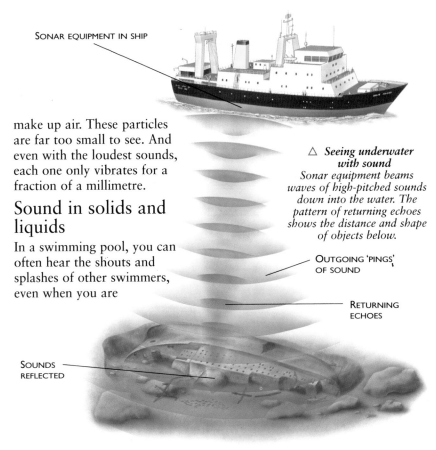

SONAR EQUIPMENT IN SHIP

make up air. These particles are far too small to see. And even with the loudest sounds, each one only vibrates for a fraction of a millimetre.

△ *Seeing underwater with sound*
Sonar equipment beams waves of high-pitched sounds down into the water. The pattern of returning echoes shows the distance and shape of objects below.

Sound in solids and liquids

In a swimming pool, you can often hear the shouts and splashes of other swimmers, even when you are

OUTGOING 'PINGS' OF SOUND

RETURNING ECHOES

SOUNDS REFLECTED

underwater. This shows that sound can travel through other substances, besides air. It can travel through solid objects, too. In fact, sound travels better through liquids and solids than it does through the air. But sound can only travel where there are particles to carry it. It cannot travel in a completely empty space, or vacuum. This is why sound cannot travel through outer space.

Finding things with echoes

Sound waves mostly bounce off solid objects. The bounced-back waves are called echoes. This happens even underwater. Sonar is a system for finding the depth of water and any objects, such as shoals of fish, submarines and wrecks on the sea bed. The time taken for the echoes to come back again shows the depth.

53

THE NATURE OF SOUND

It is difficult to imagine sound waves. We can hear them, but not see them. They are regions or ripples of high and low air pressure. The peak of the wave is really an area where the molecules of air are closer together, giving higher pressure. The trough is where the molecules are farther apart, giving low pressure.

If you could look at one place in the air as a sound wave passes by, you would see that the molecules of air are first squashed together, then stretched apart, squashed together again, and so on. This makes the air pressure at the point fall and rise. The changes happen very quickly, usually hundreds or thousands of times each second.

Speed of sound

Sound travels very fast. In normal air, it travels at about 1,240 kilometres per hour. That's more than 300 metres every second. Sound goes slightly faster when the air is warmer, and slightly slower when the air is colder.

Because sound waves travel so fast, the sound from things nearby, such as a friend talking to you, arrive at your ears almost instantly. But the farther the sound travels, the longer it takes to reach you. The time eventually becomes long enough for you to notice. For example, it takes sounds about one-quarter of a second to travel the length of a soccer pitch. Light waves travel much, much faster (see page 62),

so you see something happen before you can hear it. If a firework rocket explodes a kilometre away, the sound waves arrive at your ears about three seconds after the light waves arrive at your eyes.

Sound travels faster through liquids and solids than it does though air. For example, it goes through water five times more quickly, and through metals, such as a steel pipe, twenty times more quickly, than through air.

△ **Slower than sound**
The planes of air display teams such as the US Blue Angels can fly faster than sound. To avoid deafening the viewers, the displays are carried out at subsonic speeds.

MOLECULES CLOSE TOGETHER AT PEAK OF WAVE

Faster than sound

Objects which travel through the air faster than the speed of sound, such as fast aircraft, are called supersonic. They overtake the sounds they make, and the sounds waves from them build up into a shock wave, which you hear on the ground below as a sonic boom. The speed of supersonic aircraft is measured in Mach numbers. Mach 1 is equal to the speed of sound. Mach 2 is equal to twice the speed of sound, and so on. The fastest aircraft, such as jet fighter planes, travel at more than Mach 3.5.

◁ **Highs and lows of sound**
The way we picture sound waves, as the wavy red line, really represents areas where the molecules in air are closer together or farther apart.

MOLECULES FAR APART AT TROUGH OF WAVE

SOUND PITCH AND FREQUENCY

The deep boom of thunder is a low-pitched sound. The shrill trilling of a songbird is a high-pitched sound. The pitch of a sound depends on the number of vibrations or waves per second. This is called the frequency of sound.

△ **Changing pitch**
The keys or valves on a trumpet alter the length of the tube which air passes through, as you blow the trumpet. This makes the air and trumpet vibrate at various frequencies, giving higher and lower musical notes.

Sound's frequency is very important. Imagine it as the number of vibrations which happen every second as the sound waves go by. Sounds with higher frequencies, like a whistle or a baby crying, are higher in pitch. Sound with lower frequencies, such as the thud of a big drum or the deep roar of a big truck, are lower in pitch. Frequencies are measured in units called Hertz, Hz. One Hz is one vibration or wave per second. Our ears can hear sound of about 20 to 18,000 Hz. Sounds which are lower or

LOW PITCH (LOW FREQUENCY)

FROG

PET CAT

HUMAN

higher are all around us, but we cannot detect them. However, other animals can (see page 16). Sounds too high for our ears are known as ultrasonic, and those which are too low are infrasonic.

Echoes

Sound waves do not go on for ever. They gradually fade away, or lose energy. But sounds can bounce back off hard, smooth surfaces (see page 53). The bounced-back sounds are called echoes. You may have heard an echo from a cliff face. The farther away the cliff, the more time it takes for the echo to come back. But the weaker the echo, too, since the sound waves have lost more energy on their journey.

Acoustics

The science which studies sounds, how they are made and what they do, is called acoustics. It is very important in buildings such as concert halls and recording studios. For instance, an empty room sounds 'echoey' because sound bounces well off all of its hard walls. A room full of soft furnishings, such as chairs, carpets and curtains, does not sound echoey because the sounds do not bounce off the furnishings. Instead, they are soaked up or absorbed, so there are fewer echoes.

FACTS ABOUT SOUND

▶ The speed of sound varies with the temperature, pressure and humidity of the air it is passing through.

▶ In dry air at 0°C at sea level, sound travels at 331.5 metres per second.

▶ More water vapour in the air, that is, air which is more humid, makes sound travel faster.

▶ Increasing temperature, that is, air which is warmer, also makes sound travel faster.

▶ So in the cold, dry air at great height, sound goes more slowly, about 295 metres per second.

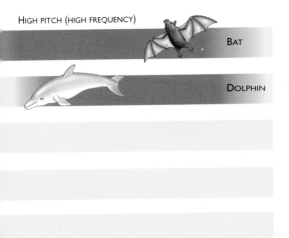

HIGH PITCH (HIGH FREQUENCY)

BAT

DOLPHIN

◁ *Hearing sounds of different pitch*
Different living things detect sounds of various pitch. The bat's squeaks are ultrasonic, far too high or shrill for most people to hear. A dolphin also hears its own very high-pitched sounds, such as whistles and clicks. A cat has a more limited range of hearing. The human range goes down to very low frequencies, less than 50 Hz. Frogs have very limited hearing indeed, mainly to hear their own croaks!

SOUND LOUDNESS AND VOLUME

The loudness of a sound depends on the height, or amplitude, of its sound waves. The higher they are, the louder the sound. Very loud sounds are dangerous and can damage our ears.

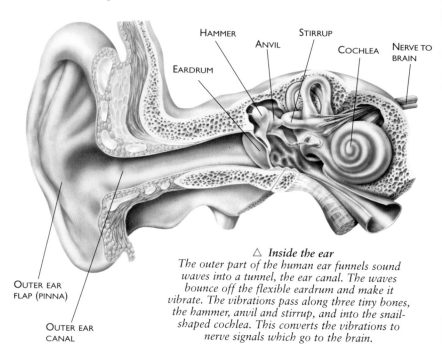

HAMMER
ANVIL
STIRRUP
COCHLEA
NERVE TO BRAIN
EARDRUM
OUTER EAR FLAP (PINNA)
OUTER EAR CANAL

△ **Inside the ear**
The outer part of the human ear funnels sound waves into a tunnel, the ear canal. The waves bounce off the flexible eardrum and make it vibrate. The vibrations pass along three tiny bones, the hammer, anvil and stirrup, and into the snail-shaped cochlea. This converts the vibrations to nerve signals which go to the brain.

TICKING WATCH
10 DB

BIRD SINGING
30 DB

TALKING QUIETLY
50 DB

SPEAKING LOUDLY
70 DB

Some sounds are so quiet you can hardly hear them. Other sounds, especially deep ones, can be so loud that you feel them hitting your body. Very loud, shrill sounds, especially, may be painful to our ears. This is important, since the pain warns us that our ears could be damaged.

The loudness or intensity of a sound is measured in decibels, dB. Normal human voices are about 40–50 decibels and heavy traffic is about 75–80 decibels.

The decibel scale does not rise in a regular step-by-step way. A rise of ten decibels means that the sound is a hundred times louder or more intense. So a noise of 70 dB is one thousand time louder than a noise of 50 dB. Heavy traffic is ten thousand times louder than a human voice.

Harmful sounds

Any sound above about 80-90 dB can harm our ears. Sound above about 110-120 dB will almost certainly do damage to the ears, causing earache, headache and loss of hearing sensitivity, especially to high-pitched sounds. The longer that the loud sounds continue, the more likely the damage, and the longer it will last. People who work in noisy places wear ear-defenders or headphones to protect their ears.

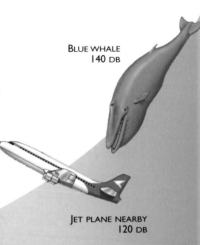

ATOMIC EXPLOSION
200 DB

▽ *How loud is quiet?*
The quietest sounds that we can hear are about 10–15 dB. Some animals, such as horses and mice, can hear sounds which are even quieter than this. Their large ears pick up and concentrate even the slightest sound waves. For these animals, a slight rustle in the grass could spell death.

BLUE WHALE
140 DB

LOUD MUSIC
85 DB

JET PLANE NEARBY
120 DB

CHAINSAW
100 DB

MUSIC AND RECORDING

The many different types of musical instruments look different, but they all make sound by vibrating the air in some way. The instruments can make sound with different frequencies and amplitudes in order to play different musical notes loudly or quietly. The sound of the instrument depends on the combinations of different sound waves that it makes.

In a stringed instrument such as a violin, the string is made to vibrate by plucking it, hitting it or sliding a bow across it. The vibrating string vibrates the air around it and also the hollow body of the violin. This sends sound waves into the surrounding air. The frequency of the sound depends on the length of the string and how tight it is. The shorter and tighter the string, the higher its note.

Wind instruments create sound with a pipe full of vibrating air. The air is set vibrating by blowing across the end of the tube, as with a flute, or by blowing over a reed to make it vibrate, as in a saxophone, or by the player vibrating his or her

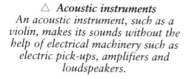

△ **Acoustic instruments**
An acoustic instrument, such as a violin, makes its sounds without the help of electrical machinery such as electric pick-ups, amplifiers and loudspeakers.

▷ **Electric instruments**
These need electrical devices, such as the guitar pick-up to be heard. This guitar is semi-acoustic, which means it has a hollow body and can be heard when strummed normally, but it also has electric pick-ups.

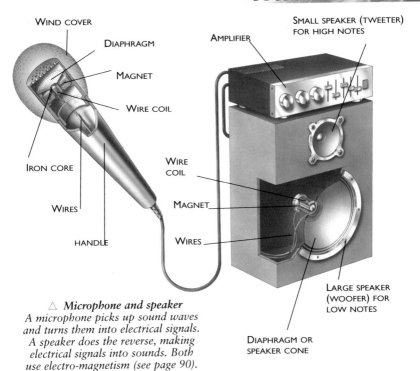

WIND COVER

DIAPHRAGM

MAGNET

WIRE COIL

IRON CORE

WIRES

HANDLE

AMPLIFIER

SMALL SPEAKER (TWEETER) FOR HIGH NOTES

WIRE COIL

MAGNET

WIRES

LARGE SPEAKER (WOOFER) FOR LOW NOTES

DIAPHRAGM OR SPEAKER CONE

△ *Microphone and speaker*
A microphone picks up sound waves and turns them into electrical signals. A speaker does the reverse, making electrical signals into sounds. Both use electro-magnetism (see page 90).

lips at the end of the tube, as with a trumpet. Changing the length of the tube (see page 56), or covering holes in the tube, changes the pitch of the note.

Percussion instruments like drums and cymbals create sounds when they vibrate after being hit.

Electric instruments

Some instruments, such as keyboards, make music using electronics instead of vibrating strings or tubes of air. In an electric guitar, the vibrations of steel strings are detected by a coil of wire, the pick-up, which makes an electrical signal. This goes to an electrical amplifier, which

makes the signals stronger. The more powerful signals can drive a loudspeaker to create very loud sounds.

Synthesized sounds

A synthesizer can actually create electrical signals which are then made into sounds. It can be adjusted to copy the sounds of almost any sort of instrument. It can also produce sounds unlike any instrument at all!

Sounds are recorded in various ways, such as patterns of magnetism on a magnetic tape, a wavy groove in a vinyl disc, or as tiny pits in a compact disc, CD (see page 73).

LIGHT AND COLOUR

Like many animals, from cats to owls, our main sense is sight. We use our eyes to find our way, look and learn, watch our surroundings and do skilled tasks such as writing and drawing. In ancient times, people's lives were dominated by light and dark. Most people were out and about during the day, using natural sunlight to see by. They slept at night, in the darkness. Today we have lights of many kinds, mostly worked by electricity, to brighten the night.

△ **All the colours**
The rainbow contains all the colours we can see.

To scientists, light is far more than something that illuminates our world. It is also a type of wave, called an electromagnetic wave (see page 64). There is a whole range of electromagnetic waves, which includes radio waves, microwaves and heat waves. Light is just one part of the range. These waves, like sound waves (see page 54), are also a form of energy.

Light goes straight

Light travels away from where it is made – a light source – in straight lines called rays. It travels incredibly fast, at 300,000 kilometres per second. Modern science says that this is the fastest that anything in the Universe can

go. Unlike sound waves, the waves of light (and other electromagnetic waves) can travel through the complete nothingness of a vacuum. So they can pass across outer space. Light rays can also bounce, or reflect, off objects and be bent, or refracted, as shown on the following pages.

Sources of light

The light that we call daylight comes from the Sun. It is given off by the incredibly hot gases at the Sun's surface (see page 102). Even though light goes so fast, the Sun is so far away that its light takes more than eight minutes to reach Earth.

Very hot or burning things also create light. For example, a

△ *Seeing a colourful scene*
Almost wherever we look, we see an
amazingly complicated and intricate
pattern of shapes, colours, shadows,
reflections and refractions, all created
by light waves.

FACTS ABOUT LIGHT

▶ Light travels at ... the speed of light! This is almost exactly 300,000 kilometres per second.

▶ The speed of light is so fast that it can travel around the Earth seven times in less than a second.

▶ All the waves which are similar to light, called electromagnetic waves, go at the same speed.

▶ But this is the speed of light in a vacuum, or nothingness. Air is so thin that the speed of light in air is almost the same as its speed in a vacuum.

▶ In substances such as water and glass, light travels more slowly.

flame gives off light. A candle or oil lamp burns with a yellowish-white glow. The light from a light bulb comes from the very thin, hot, glowing wire inside the bulb, which has electricity flowing through it. In a fluorescent light tube, light is made by a gas inside the tube that makes the inside coating of the tube glow brightly.

THE NATURE OF LIGHT

Light and other electromagnetic waves are a combined form of energy. They are both electrical and magnetic (see page 90). Imagine an upright wave of energy which is electrical, going up and down in strength. Then picture a wave of magnetism which does the same, along with the electrical wave, but which lies on its side compared to the electrical wave. This is an electromagnetic wave.

Light can pass through some substances, but not through others. For instance, you can see through the glass in a window, but not through the wall next to it. This is because light is affected in different ways by different materials. Some substances let all the light that hits them go straight through. They are called transparent materials. Glass is transparent. So is air, and water. Through a transparent material, you can see clearly any objects on the other side.

Opaque and translucent

Some substances do not let any light pass through them. They are called opaque materials. The light either disappears into the material or it bounces off it, as a reflection. You cannot see anything on the other side of an opaque object. Brick, wood and metal are opaque materials.

Some substances let light

▽ *The range of electromagnetic waves*
The EMS (electromagnetic spectrum)
covers a huge range. The waves differ
only in their lengths, and their frequency
or numbers per second. Radio waves are
very long, some being many kilometres
in length. X-rays are extremely short,
with billions in one centimetre.

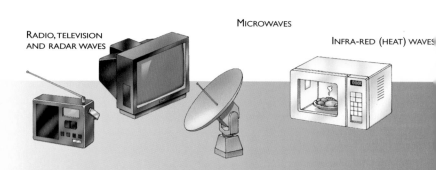

RADIO, TELEVISION AND RADAR WAVES

MICROWAVES

INFRA-RED (HEAT) WAVES

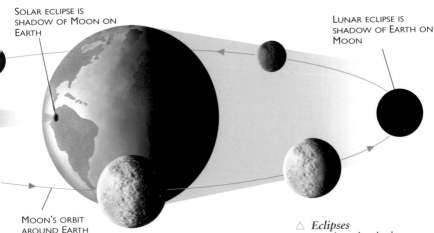

SOLAR ECLIPSE IS
SHADOW OF MOON ON
EARTH

LUNAR ECLIPSE IS
SHADOW OF EARTH ON
MOON

MOON'S ORBIT
AROUND EARTH

△ *Eclipses*
An eclipse happens when the shadow of the Earth falls on the Moon, which is called a lunar eclipse. Or the shadow of the Moon falls on the Earth, which is known as a solar eclipse. During a solar eclipse, the Sun is blocked out by the Moon for a few minutes, so that on Earth, it goes dark – like night.

through, but they scatter the waves about. You can see the general brightness of light coming through the material, but you cannot see things on the other side clearly. These materials are translucent. A glass of milky water and frosted·glass are translucent.

Making shadows

Where light waves are stopped by an opaque object, there is a patch of darkness on the other side. This is called a shadow. On a sunny day, you can see your shadow as a sharp-edged dark area. It is there because light is coming directly from the Sun in straight lines, and none of the waves can go through your body. On an overcast day, the clouds scatter the Sun's rays, so they come from all directions. So you do not see a shadow with clear, sharp edges.

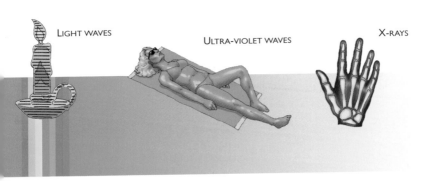

LIGHT WAVES

ULTRA-VIOLET WAVES

X-RAYS

REFLECTIONS

REFLECTIONS

We can see our surroundings because light from them enters our eyes. The eye detects the light and sends information about it to the brain (see page 17). Most of the things we see do not make light themselves. Instead, light rays from a source of light bounce off them into our eyes. This bouncing of light is called reflection.

Different objects and materials look different to us because of the way light rays bounce off them. Very flat surfaces, such as metal, glass, gloss paint, glazed pottery and the plastic-coated cover of this book, look shiny and glinting because they reflect most of the light that hits them, back in the same direction that it came.

Dull surfaces, such as cloth and newspaper, do not shine or glint because they scatter the light rays that hit them.

Mirrors

A mirror has a surface which reflects all the light that hits it. Also, it reflects this light exactly, bouncing it back in the same

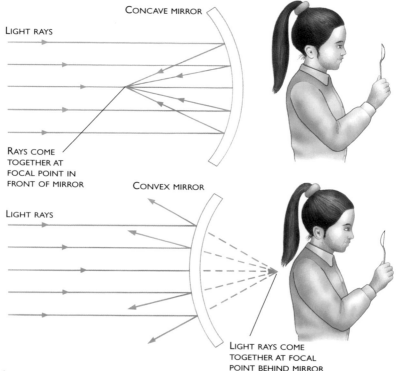

CONCAVE MIRROR

LIGHT RAYS

RAYS COME TOGETHER AT FOCAL POINT IN FRONT OF MIRROR

CONVEX MIRROR

LIGHT RAYS

LIGHT RAYS COME TOGETHER AT FOCAL POINT BEHIND MIRROR

△ **Mirror of water**
The flat water surface of a calm lake works as a mirror, to reflect the scene above it almost perfectly.

IMAGE IS UPSIDE DOWN
AND DISTORTED

IMAGE IS RIGHT WAY UP
AND DISTORTED

pattern that it arrives at the mirror. So it appears that anything in front of mirror is behind it too.

Most mirrors are made from glass with a very shiny, silvery paint on the back surface. The light goes through the glass, bounces off the smooth surface of the paint, and passes back out through the glass again.

Curved mirrors

A normal mirror is flat. But there are also curved mirrors. A mirror which is convex, or bulging, makes the image in it look bigger, or magnified. Convex mirrors are used in shaving and make-up mirrors, and car wing and rear-view mirrors.

◁ **Curved mirrors**
A shiny spoon works as a mirror on both sides. The bulging or convex side produces a magnified and distorted (out-of-shape) reflection. The concave or bowl-shaped side does the same and also turns the image upside down.

67

REFRACTION

At the swimming pool, swimmers under the water look their normal shape when the water is calm. But they look wobbly when there are waves on the water. This happens because light rays change direction when they move from water to air. This effect is called refraction.

Refraction happens whenever light passes from one transparent material, or medium, to another. This may be from air to glass, or from glass to water, or from clear plastic to air. The rays are bent or

△ *Under the microscope*
In a microscope (see opposite), two or more convex lenses work together to make tiny objects seem much bigger. The micro-photograph above shows the tiny hairs on the surface of an insect, magnified about 200 times.

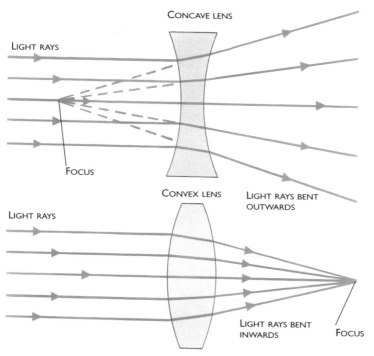

CONCAVE LENS

LIGHT RAYS

FOCUS

LIGHT RAYS BENT OUTWARDS

CONVEX LENS

LIGHT RAYS

LIGHT RAYS BENT INWARDS

FOCUS

refracted by a certain angle. This angle depends on the two types of media and is known as the index of refraction.

Lenses are curved pieces of transparent substance, such as glass or clear plastic. They bend or refract light in an organized way, to produce a clear image – but an image which is changed in some way.

Convex lenses

A convex lens has faces which curve outwards, so that the lens is thicker in the middle than at the edges. It bends all light rays coming from a point on one side so that they meet up at a point on the other side. This is called focusing. Convex lenses are the types of lens in magnifying glasses, telescopes and microscopes. They can make things look bigger than they really are, because they bend the light rays from an object inwards, making them seem to come from a bigger object.

Concave lenses

The other common type of lens is a concave lens. It has faces which curve inwards, making the centre of the lens thinner than the

edges. It bends light from an object outwards. It makes an object look smaller because it bends the light rays from it out, so that they seem to come from a smaller object.

▽ *Inside a microscope*
A microscope has several sets of lenses. Those nearest the object being examined are objective lenses. They are curved by different amounts and can be changed to give different magnifications, usually up to about one thousand times real size.

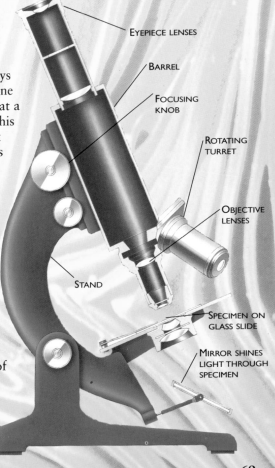

EYEPIECE LENSES

BARREL

FOCUSING KNOB

ROTATING TURRET

OBJECTIVE LENSES

STAND

SPECIMEN ON GLASS SLIDE

MIRROR SHINES LIGHT THROUGH SPECIMEN

COLOURS OF LIGHT

W e see colours because of light. The light from the Sun and from light bulbs is called white light. It is made from a range of different colours of light mixed together. The range of colours is called the colour spectrum.

Sometimes, we see the whole colour spectrum, from red light, through yellow and green, to blue and violet. This happens when white sunlight is split up, for example, by raindrops in the sky. The result is called a rainbow.

Light is in different colours because of its wavelength (see page 64). The longest waves of visible light are red in colour. The medium-length waves are green.

The shortest waves are violet. Waves which are shorter than this are called ultraviolet. We cannot see them, because they are outside the visible light spectrum which our eyes can detect. But they sometimes affect us because ultraviolet rays from the Sun can cause sunburn. Similarly, waves which are longer than those of red light are called infra-red. Again, we cannot see them, but we feel their heating effects.

Using colour

Different colours have different meanings and affect our thoughts and feelings. We think of red and yellow as 'warm'. Blue and green are

WHITE SUNLIGHT

RAINDROP WORKS AS TINY PRISM

LIGHT REFRACTED INTO COLOURS OF SPECTRUM

◁ *Seeing the rainbow*
In a rainstorm, millions of tiny raindrops act as prisms to split the white light of the Sun into its separate colours. The colours come together and reach our eyes as a rainbow.

'cool'. Also, some colours have special meanings in communication. For example, reds and yellows are often used in warning symbols, such as on road signs.

Animals use colours, too. For example, many male birds have coloured feathers for courtship displays, while bees and wasps have yellow stripes to warn of their stings.

Colour filters

The light from a normal light bulb is white light. So how can some light bulbs make coloured light? The answer is that the glass is coloured or tinted. The tint stops all the colours from leaving the bulb, except for the required one. So a red bulb has red tinted glass that stops all the colours of the spectrum from passing through, except red.

△ **Splitting light**
A prism is an angled transparent block that refracts the various wavelengths, or colours, of light by different amounts. So the mixture of wavelengths in white light is split up, and we can see the various colours separately. They are usually listed as red (with the longest waves), orange, yellow, green, blue, indigo and violet (with the shortest waves).

71

USING LIGHT

Light, like all types of electromagnetic waves, is a form of energy. We can trap or catch this energy in various ways and use it for many purposes. Sunlight, in particular, is a renewable form of energy that will last for millions of years. Plants also trap light energy, by photosynthesis (see page 9), and this is another useful energy source.

Sunlight is a free and non-polluting form of energy. We can trap it using solar panels, which convert the energy in light into electrical energy. However, the energy in sunlight is relatively weak and spread out over huge areas. Strong sunlight is also irregular, except in certain places which have hot, bright, sunny days over most of the year. And it is not available at night.

Laser light

Have you ever been to a big event such as a music concert or theatre performance, where there has been a laser display? A laser beam is a special kind of light. It is very powerful and intense, with lots of

▽ **Solar power**
Solar panels turn the Sun's light energy into electricity. But for usefully large amounts of electricity, the panels must cover huge areas.

▽ The laser CD player
A compact disc, CD, is 'read' by a tiny red laser beam. The beam shines at the disc's mirror surface and reflects back again to a light sensor. Except where there are tiny holes or pits in the disc's surface, when there is no reflection. The pattern of reflections contains information in coded form.

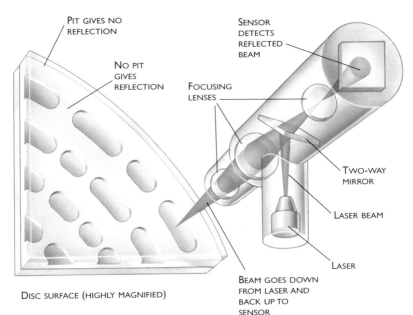

PIT GIVES NO REFLECTION

NO PIT GIVES REFLECTION

SENSOR DETECTS REFLECTED BEAM

FOCUSING LENSES

TWO-WAY MIRROR

LASER BEAM

LASER

BEAM GOES DOWN FROM LASER AND BACK UP TO SENSOR

DISC SURFACE (HIGHLY MAGNIFIED)

energy. It contains only one pure colour rather than a mixture of colours. Its waves are all in step, rising and falling together, rather than being out of step as in normal light. And laser light does not spread out like an ordinary torch beam. A laser beam is made by a device called a laser.

Useful lasers

Lasers are not just for making pretty displays. They are important tools in industry, medicine and communications.

Powerful lasers can cut very accurately through metals and other materials. Low-power lasers are used for delicate surgery, such as eye operations. Flashes of laser light are sent along fibre-optic cables, to carry information such as telephone calls and computer data in coded form. Lasers are also used in CD players, and in supermarket check-outs for reading bar codes on products. But laser light is powerful and can be dangerous. Never look directly at a laser or at the Sun.

ENERGY, FORCE
AND MOTION

When you feel tired, you might complain that you have no energy – not even to move. Energy lets you do things, such as walking to school or playing a game. In fact, nothing can happen without energy. For example, household gadgets would not work, cars would not move along the road, and even the weather would grind to a standstill.

◁ *Potential energy*
The downward pull of the Earth's gravity gives things potential energy. We can measure this as the weight, or mass, of an object, by its pull on a spring balance.

▽ *Kinetic energy*
Movement represents a form of energy, called kinetic energy. A speeding train seems like a large amount of this type of energy. But a volcanic eruption or earthquake is many millions of times more powerful.

There are many different forms of energy. They include sound waves, and light, radio and all the other kinds of electromagnetic waves.

In fact, all waves and rays are forms of energy. Also, they can carry or transfer energy from the place they are made to the places which they reach.

When you feel the Sun's warmth and see by its light, you are receiving energy made in the Sun which has travelled across many millions of kilometres of empty space.

△ Releasing energy
When something burns, the chemical energy stored in its molecules is turned into light and heat.

Other forms of energy

Electricity is also energy (see page 90). It is a very useful form because it can be sent along wires and easily controlled. There is energy in objects, too. Any object which is moving has movement or kinetic energy.

Storing energy

Energy can be stored, for use later. Chemical energy is in molecules, stored as the links or bonds between the atoms of the molecules. In substances such as coal, oil and other fuels, this energy is released when the fuel is burned. Electricity can be stored in chemical form, inside a rechargeable battery. There are other forms of stored energy, too, such as the energy stored in a stretched elastic band, or in the water behind a dam which is tying to flow downstream.

75

FORCE OF GRAVITY

What goes up must come down! According to the law of gravity, that is. Gravity is a force which pulls all objects towards the centre of the Earth. In fact, gravity pulls every object towards every other object, no matter how big or small they are. This includes you pulling this book towards yourself – and the book pulling you towards it.

△ **Zero gravity**
About 200 kilometres above the Earth's surface, an astronaut floats through space. The Earth's gravity is so weak at this height that the astronaut has no weight at all. The pull of gravity is zero – 'zero g'.

Every object, even as tiny as an atom, has gravitational pull. But the force of gravity is only noticeable when one or both of the objects is very massive – as big as a star or planet.

Mass and weight

Here on Earth, the weight of an object is a measure of how much the Earth's gravity pulls it towards the centre of the Earth. Weight is a force, and so it is measured in units called newtons (see page 83).

However, in everyday life, when we ask the weight of something, we get an answer in grams and kilograms, or in pounds and ounces.

In strict scientific terms, this measure of weight is not really correct. The kilogram is a measure of a different type of effect, which is called mass. The mass of an object is a measure of how much matter there is in it, in terms of the numbers and types of atoms and molecules.

Mass does not vary as you travel around the Universe. But weight does vary, with the pull of gravity of huge nearby objects. For example, if your mass is 25 kilograms, it is 25 kilograms on Earth, and on the Moon, and in deep space.

But your weight depends on the pull of gravity. So it would be about 250 newtons here on Earth, about 40 newtons on the Moon (which has one-sixth of the Earth's gravity), and zero newtons in deep space.

Gravity in space

The force of gravity between two objects quickly gets smaller, the farther apart the objects are. If you travelled 5,000 kilometres above the Earth's surface, you would weigh as much as you would on the Moon, because the Earth's gravity so far out has lessened to only one-quarter of its value at the Earth's surface.

In deep space, you are so far from any large gravity-pulling body, that you are weightless. But not mass-less.

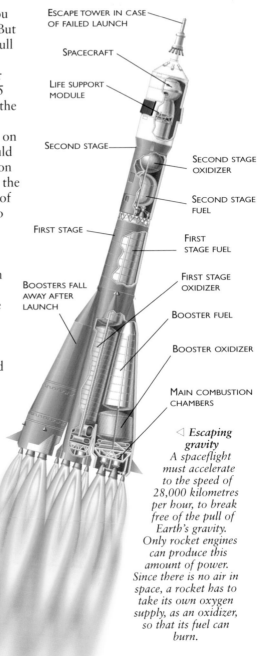

ESCAPE TOWER IN CASE OF FAILED LAUNCH

SPACECRAFT

LIFE SUPPORT MODULE

SECOND STAGE

SECOND STAGE OXIDIZER

SECOND STAGE FUEL

FIRST STAGE

FIRST STAGE FUEL

FIRST STAGE OXIDIZER

BOOSTERS FALL AWAY AFTER LAUNCH

BOOSTER FUEL

BOOSTER OXIDIZER

MAIN COMBUSTION CHAMBERS

◁ *Escaping gravity*
A spaceflight must accelerate to the speed of 28,000 kilometres per hour, to break free of the pull of Earth's gravity. Only rocket engines can produce this amount of power. Since there is no air in space, a rocket has to take its own oxygen supply, as an oxidizer, so that its fuel can burn.

EXHAUST GASES BLAST OUT AS FLAMES AND SMOKE

CONVERTING ENERGY

The amount of energy in the Universe has always been the same, since the beginning of time. Energy cannot be created or destroyed. When we say that energy is 'used', it does not disappear. It is changed or converted into other forms of energy.

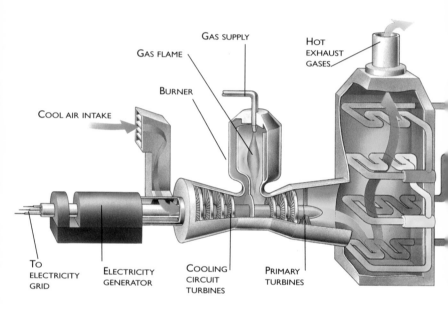

GAS SUPPLY

GAS FLAME

HOT EXHAUST GASES

BURNER

COOL AIR INTAKE

TO ELECTRICITY GRID

ELECTRICITY GENERATOR

COOLING CIRCUIT TURBINES

PRIMARY TURBINES

Energy is changing from one form to another all the time. Think of an everyday activity, such as typing on a computer keyboard. Where does the energy come from to make the letters appear on the screen? Firstly, energy is needed to make your fingers press the keys. This movement energy comes from the energy stored in your body, as blood sugars (glucose). This came from the chemical energy in food. And this energy came originally from sunlight, which was captured by plants and eaten by animals.

Electrical energy is needed to make the computer work. This energy comes from a power or electricity-generating station. It was obtained from some kind of fuel. This may be the movement or kinetic energy of flowing water in a hydroelectric power station. Or it may be from burning coal, gas, oil or other fossil fuels (see below). The fossil fuels were made from plants, animals and

▽ **Energy changes in a power station**
In a gas-fired power station, one form of energy – the chemical links or bonds in gas molecules – is burned to give off light and heat energy, as huge flames. The heat warms up a heat-exchange fluid flowing through pipes. Hot gases are also produced, which have kinetic (movement) energy. *They rush past fan-like primary turbine blades and make them spin around. The blades are connected by a shaft to an electricity generator. Meanwhile the heat-exchange fluid carries its warmth to the main turbines. These also spin around and turn their own generator, to make more electricity. The whole process involves energy changing from chemical, to heat, to movement, to electrical.*

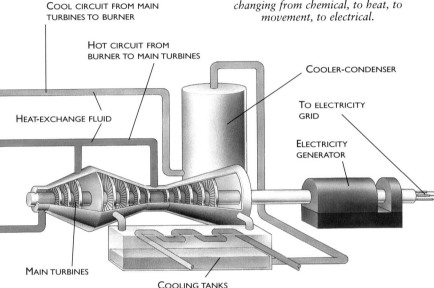

COOL CIRCUIT FROM MAIN TURBINES TO BURNER

HOT CIRCUIT FROM BURNER TO MAIN TURBINES

COOLER-CONDENSER

HEAT-EXCHANGE FLUID

TO ELECTRICITY GRID

ELECTRICITY GENERATOR

MAIN TURBINES

COOLING TANKS

other organisms, which also got their energy from the Sun!

Work and power

When scientists talk about work being done, they mean that energy is being converted from one form to another, such as movement to electricity. The measure of work is the total amount of energy which has been converted.

Power is how fast the energy is converted, in a certain time.

FACTS ABOUT ENERGY

▶ Sound is a relatively weak form of energy. If you could collect all the sound energy at a huge sports event, like a soccer match, and convert it into heat energy, it would be only enough to boil one kettle of water.

▶ Matter, or atoms and molecules, represent incredibly concentrated forms of energy. A nuclear power station converts atoms of uranium into smaller atoms and gigantic amounts of energy. A fist-sized lump of uranium provides as much energy as a week's output of coal from one large coal mine.

HEAT AND COLD

Heat and temperature are often confused. To a scientist, they are not the same thing. Heat is a form of energy. It is measured, like all forms of energy, in joules. Temperature is a measure of how much heat something contains – that is, how hot it is. This is measured in degrees Celsius (°C).

When you watch a fire, you see yellowish flames, tiny red-hot sparks, and glowing coal or wood. The fuel, flames and sparks glow because they are so hot. They are at a very high temperature. As the sparks drift away from the fire, they quickly stop glowing in a second or two, because they lose heat and become cooler.

Compare this idea of heat and temperature with the idea of a warm drink. It is much cooler than the sparks of a fire. So it does not glow. But it takes much longer to go cold, perhaps ten minutes, compared to the sparks. The temperature of the sparks is much higher than the temperature of the drink. But the drink contains much more heat than the sparks.

Heat energy rarely stays in the same place for long. It always tries to spread out evenly, and move from hotter to cooler places. For example, a hot drink

▽ **Hot and runny**
Lava from a volcano is rock that is so hot, oozing up from the depths of the Earth, that it has melted. It flows like a thick liquid. As it loses heat, it goes solid again.

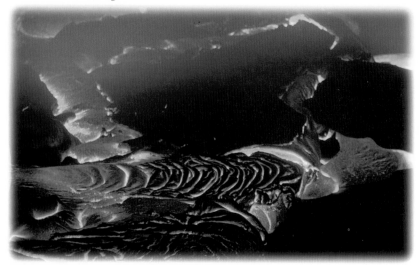

▷ *What is heat?*
Heat is the to-and-fro movements, or vibrations, of atoms and molecules in a substance. In a very hot substance, they move a lot (top). At room temperature, the movements are less (middle). In an intensely cold substance, the movements almost cease (bottom)

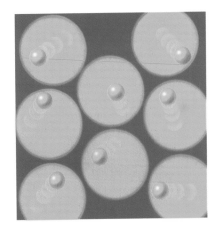

gradually cools down because heat moves from it, into the cooler air around it.

How heat moves

Heat moves and spreads in three main ways. It can move through solid materials by conduction. The particles or molecules of the substance pass their heat energy from one to the next. Materials which conduct heat well, such as metals, are called thermal conductors. Materials which do not conduct heat well, such as plastics and woods, are called thermal insulators.

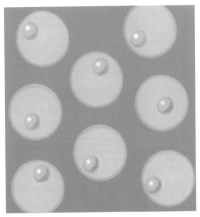

In gases and liquids, heat moves by convection. When one part of the gas or liquid is heated, it expands (gets bigger). It floats upwards, carrying the heat with it, and is replaced by cooler gas or liquid from below. The pattern of moving gas or liquid is called a convection current.

Heat also moves by radiation. This involves giving off infra-red rays, part of the electromagnetic spectrum (see page 64). Conduction and convection can only pass through substances or matter. But radiation can go through empty space.

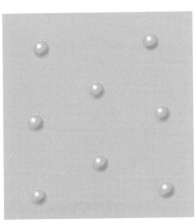

FORCES

A force is a simple thing. It is a push, pull or shove on an object. A force can have different effects. It can make an object start moving, make it speed up or slow down, cause it to stop, or 'force' it to change direction. We can predict what a force will do, according to Newton's laws of motion, devised by famous scientist Isaac Newton.

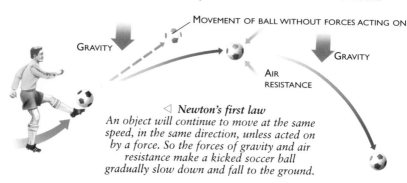

MOVEMENT OF BALL WITHOUT FORCES ACTING ON

GRAVITY

GRAVITY

AIR RESISTANCE

◁ *Newton's first law*
An object will continue to move at the same speed, in the same direction, unless acted on by a force. So the forces of gravity and air resistance make a kicked soccer ball gradually slow down and fall to the ground.

Two forces acting together can have different effects to one force alone. They can squash or stretch an object, make it begin to spin, make it turn faster, or cause its spinning to slow or stop. Three or more forces can twist or bend an object.

The bigger the forces, the greater the effects they have. Energy and forces are closely linked. Energy is always needed to make a force, and when the force acts on an object, energy is always transferred to or from the object. Some forces have special names, such as friction (see page 86) and gravity (see page 76).

ACTION – BALLS COME TOGETHER

REACTION – BALLS BOUNCE APART

◁ *Newton's second law*
The effect of a force is in proportion to its strength or magnitude. The harder the ball is kicked, the faster and farther it goes.

△ *Newton's third law*
For every action, there is an equal and opposite reaction. So if two balls roll together and hit each other, they rebound apart again.

SOFT TAP

HARD KICK

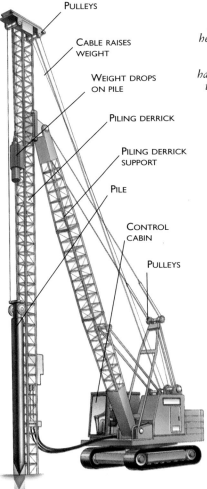

PULLEYS

CABLE RAISES
WEIGHT

WEIGHT DROPS
ON PILE

PILING DERRICK

PILING DERRICK
SUPPORT

PILE

CONTROL
CABIN

PULLEYS

PILE
DRIVEN
IN

◁ *Transferring force*
A piledriver is a machine that drops a heavy weight repeatedly onto a large rod-shaped pile. The force of the falling weight is transferred to the pile and hammers it into the ground. Piles are used to support buildings, bridges and other large structures.

Action and reaction

Have you ever noticed that when you push on an object, the object seems to push back? Scientists call this force a reaction. It is always the same size as the force you make, but it always pushes in the opposite direction.

This effect is known as action-reaction. It is explained in Newton's third law. Newton's first two laws explain the basic workings of motion and forces. They were devised by physicist and mathematician Isaac Newton more than three hundred years ago. Newton's ideas are still used by scientists and engineers today. However in certain types of science, such as space travel, the more accurate and wider-ranging ideas of Albert Einstein have replaced Newton's laws.

FACTS ABOUT FORCES
MEASURING FORCES

▶ The size of a force is measured in newtons, in honour of the English scientist Isaac Newton.

▶ One newton is defined as the force needed to make an object with the mass of one kilogram increase its speed of movement by one metre per second, each second.

▶ The force needed to hold up an object weighing about 100 grams (such as an orange), against the downwards pull of gravity, is about one newton.

ON THE MOVE

When you are in a hurry to get somewhere, you want to travel as fast as possible – at top speed. But what, in scientific terms, is speed?

▷ *Speeding around bends*
Objects tend to move in straight lines. To move in a curve requires a force pushing the object from the side. To counteract this force, a motorcyclist leans into the curve, to avoid toppling over.

Speed is the distance that something travels in a certain time. For example, walking speed is about five kilometres per hour. This means, if you kept walking for an hour, you would cover about five kilometres.

Velocity is slightly different from speed. Velocity includes the speed at which an object is moving, and also the direction it is moving in. So the speed of a passenger jet plane taking people on holiday may be around 1,000 kilometres per hour. But its velocity is 1,000 kilometres per hour heading due west.

Average speed

The average speed of a journey is the total distance you travel, divided by the total time that the journey took. For example, if you travelled 100 kilometres in two hours, you would have

SPINNING SHAFT

FRAME

SPINNING WHEEL

CONE-SHAPED BEARING

◁ *Staying steady*
A gyroscope has a heavy, rapidly spinning wheel which tends to stay steady and resist attempts to tilt or twist it. Gyroscopes are used in planes, rockets, missiles, ships and similar fast-moving objects

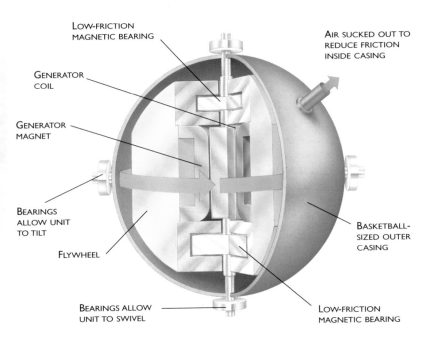

LOW-FRICTION
MAGNETIC BEARING

AIR SUCKED OUT TO
REDUCE FRICTION
INSIDE CASING

GENERATOR
COIL

GENERATOR
MAGNET

BEARINGS
ALLOW UNIT
TO TILT

FLYWHEEL

BASKETBALL-
SIZED OUTER
CASING

BEARINGS ALLOW
UNIT TO SWIVEL

LOW-FRICTION
MAGNETIC BEARING

△ *Storing the energy of movement*
A flywheel is a large, heavy wheel that needs lots of
energy to get it moving, but then keeps moving for a
long time. A modern hi-tech version with a
generator inside could be used to produce electricity.

travelled at an average speed of
50 kilometres per hour – even
though you might have travelled
faster for some parts of the
journey, and stopped about half
way for a short break.

Speed up, slow down

Going faster is called acceleration.
Slowing down is deceleration. A
force is always needed to make an
object accelerate or decelerate.
For example, when you throw a
ball, you push on the back of the
ball, speeding it up until you let
go. When you catch a ball, you

push on the ball again, this time
decelerating it to bring it to a
stop. The larger the force, the
greater is the acceleration or
deceleration, so the quicker the
ball speeds up or slows down.

Spinning round

Turning or spinning around is
similar to moving along. Think
about spinning a bicycle wheel
round. A push on the wheel
makes it go round faster, and a
pull makes it slow down again.
Without any force, the wheel
keeps spinning at the same speed.

FRICTION AND PRESSURE

Try a simple experiment. Slide this book across a smooth table-top. (Gently!) The book soon comes to a stop. It has decelerated, so there must be a force at work. This force is friction. It tries to stop surfaces sliding past each other, so it acts between the book and the table, to slow down the book.

Friction is sometimes useful to us, and sometimes a menace. For example, on a bicycle, friction between the tyres and the road surface helps you to grip the road. Friction between the brake blocks and wheel rim slows the bicycle down when you operate the brakes.

But friction also tries to stop the wheels turning on their axles, which would slow you down and make pedalling hard. However, the wheels have specially designed ball bearings and slippery lubricating grease, to reduce friction to a minimum.

Friction in fluids

Friction also tries to slow down any object moving through a fluid (a gas or a liquid). In this case it is often called drag (see page 40). The faster the object moves, the bigger drag becomes. Also, the thicker or denser the fluid, the bigger drag becomes. So running through air, a very thin fluid, is much easier than running through water, which is a thicker, denser fluid.

Pressure

Pressure is closely related to force. It is the amount of force which presses on a certain area. Pressure is measured in newtons per square metre. Objects with sharp points, such as pins and nails, are easy to push into materials because the force on them is concentrated into a very small area, making a very high pressure. Blunter objects are difficult to push in because the pressure they

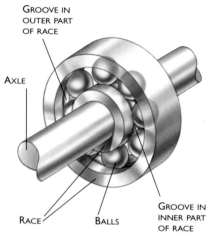

GROOVE IN
OUTER PART
OF RACE

AXLE

GROOVE IN
INNER PART
OF RACE

RACE   BALLS

◁ **Inside a ball bearing**
The bearing contains a number of very hard, smooth, steel balls held in place by a collar-shaped race. As the axle turns, the balls turn too, lessening friction to almost zero.

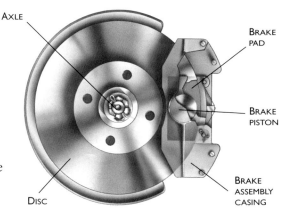

AXLE

BRAKE PAD

BRAKE PISTON

BRAKE ASSEMBLY CASING

DISC

make is much lower. For example, it is easy to push the sharp edge of a spade into the soil, but much more difficult to push the flat sole of a boot into the same soil.

Fluids can exert pressure, too. They can press along tubes and pipes, as in hydraulic and pneumatic machines. Pressure and friction, working together in a car's brakes, can make a car slow down rapidly.

△▽ *How car disc brakes work*
The brake has a large metal disc that turns around with the road wheel. To slow the spinning disc, and make the car slow down, pads press on it from either side. The pads are worked by hydraulic pressure – fluid being pushed along the brake pipe and pressing on the pistons, which push the pads.

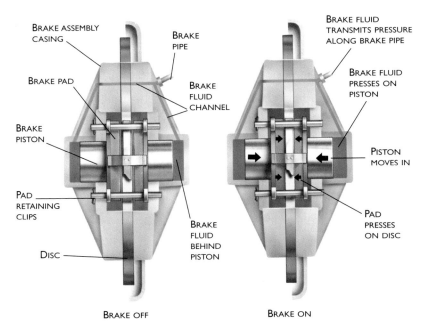

BRAKE ASSEMBLY CASING

BRAKE PIPE

BRAKE PAD

BRAKE FLUID CHANNEL

BRAKE PISTON

PAD RETAINING CLIPS

DISC

BRAKE FLUID BEHIND PISTON

BRAKE OFF

BRAKE FLUID TRANSMITS PRESSURE ALONG BRAKE PIPE

BRAKE FLUID PRESSES ON PISTON

PISTON MOVES IN

PAD PRESSES ON DISC

BRAKE ON

87

MACHINES

A machine is a device which makes life easier for us. Most machines have several parts, some of which might move. Some machines, such as robots and submarines, are very complex. Scientists also think of simple tools, such as spades and scissors, as machines, too.

◁ *Machine-like structures*
A building is a structure, rather than a true machine. But scientists and engineers use the same mechanical principles they would use when designing a real machine, involving forces, pressures, wedges and levers.

There are several types of simple machines which help us to lift or move things. They include the sloping surface (inclined plane), the wedge (which is two inclined planes back-to-back), the wheel and pulley, and various kinds of levers.

Planes and screws

Walking up a steep hill on a zig-zag path is easier than walking straight up the slope. This is because less effort is needed to walk up a gradual slope than a steep one. The slope, also called a

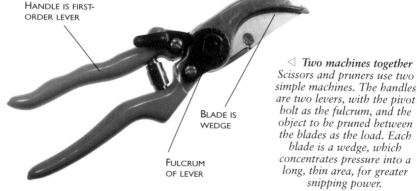

HANDLE IS FIRST-ORDER LEVER

BLADE IS WEDGE

FULCRUM OF LEVER

◁ *Two machines together*
Scissors and pruners use two simple machines. The handles are two levers, with the pivot bolt as the fulcrum, and the object to be pruned between the blades as the load. Each blade is a wedge, which concentrates pressure into a long, thin area, for greater snipping power.

ramp or inclined plane, is acting as a simple machine. However, you have to walk farther up the zig-zag path to reach the top, than you do if you walk straight up the steep hillside. This shows a very important principle of machines. They make tasks easier, but overall, they do not save any energy or effort, or give us something for nothing.

The screw is like a wedge wrapped around itself, in a corkscrew or helix shape. In a typical woodscrew, the turns of the screw part, or thread, also get wider as they go up the screw. They increase in diameter. So the woodscrew thread is a combination of helix and spiral. In a bolt, the diameter of the thread stays the same.

Wheels

A wheel is a disc or circular object that spins around. Most wheels spin on a central rod, called an axle. A wheel works in the same way as an inclined plane or ramp. It is like an inclined plane that goes on for ever, wrapped around a central point.

Pulleys

The pulley is a simple machine which makes a pull bigger. The simplest version is a wheel with a rope around it, hanging down on either side. Pulling down on one end of the rope pulls the load on the other end upwards.

Most pulleys have more than one wheel. The greater the number of wheels, the more the pull is magnified and the easier lifting is. But again, as with levers, you do not get something for nothing. You need to pull a greater length of rope to lift the load by the same amount.

▽ **Types of levers**
A lever is a stiff rod or beam which pivots around a fixed point, the fulcrum. Pushing or pulling on one part of the rod makes it swivel around the pivot. This makes a larger or smaller force at the other end, to lift or move an object. The force you make is the effort. The object moved is the load. There are three types, or orders, of levers.

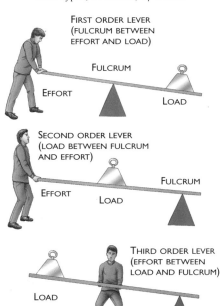

FIRST ORDER LEVER
(FULCRUM BETWEEN EFFORT AND LOAD)

FULCRUM

EFFORT

LOAD

SECOND ORDER LEVER
(LOAD BETWEEN FULCRUM AND EFFORT)

FULCRUM

EFFORT

LOAD

THIRD ORDER LEVER
(EFFORT BETWEEN LOAD AND FULCRUM)

LOAD

EFFORT

FULCRUM

ELECTRICITY AND MAGNETISM

How many electrical machines and devices do you use every day? Probably more than you think. Look around and count how many things work with electricity. They are the machines which are plugged into a wall socket, or which need batteries. They range from simple gadgets like light bulbs and electric heaters, to those with electric motors such as food mixers and battery-operated toys, to complex electronic machines like televisions, computers and hi-fis. Electricity is vital to our modern world. It is also closely linked to one of nature's most mysterious forces – magnetism

What is electricity? It involves electrons, the tiny particles which make up the outer parts of atoms (see page 22). An electric current is a stream of electrons moving from one place to another. In some materials, the electrons can move easily from one atom to the next. So electricity flows easily through them. They are called conductors. Most conductors are metals, such as iron and copper. Other materials have electrons which are stuck firmly to their

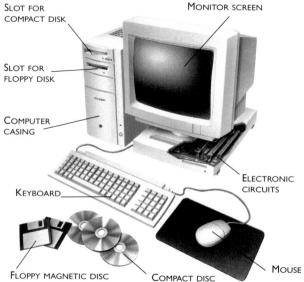

SLOT FOR COMPACT DISK

MONITOR SCREEN

SLOT FOR FLOPPY DISK

COMPUTER CASING

KEYBOARD

ELECTRONIC CIRCUITS

FLOPPY MAGNETIC DISC

COMPACT DISC

MOUSE

◁ **Electric or electronic?** *Usually, an electrical machine is one with obvious moving parts, such as a washing machine or electric train. An electronic machine such as a calculator or computer has few or no moving parts – at least, to our eyes. There are moving parts, of course. But these are electrons, which are far too small for us to see.*

atoms and cannot move about. Electricity cannot pass through them easily. These substances are called insulators.

Static electricity

An electric current cannot pass through a good insulating material. But rubbing two insulating materials together, such as rubber and cloth, can make electrons 'jump' from one material to the other. The material which gains electrons gains a negative electric charge, because electrons themselves are negative. The material which loses electrons is left with a lack of negative electrons, so it has a

△ *The power of electricity*
A bolt of lightning is a gigantic spark of electricity passing though the air, from thunderclouds to the ground (or the other way). It contains enough power to supply a small town with electricity for half a year.

positive electric charge. These two opposite electrical charges attract each other with a small force. This is why, if you pass a plastic comb through your hair, the strands seem to stick to the comb. If the charges are large enough, a spark jumps from one material to the other. The spark is a split-second stream of electrons, evening out the charges again.

ELECTRIC CIRCUITS

An electric current can only flow if there is a pathway for the electrons to pass along, and something pushing them. The pushing force is provided by a battery or the mains electricity supply. The pathway is provided by a loop of conducting material, such as wires or strips of metal. The loop is called an electric circuit.

If you fold a piece of wire into a loop, you have made a circuit. But an electric current does not flow around it. You need a supply of electrons and a force to push them along. This is called a potential difference. A battery makes a potential difference. It works in a similar way to a pump in a loop of hose pipe, which pushes water around the loop.

There is a simple circuit inside a torch. The batteries are a store of electricity, and they make the potential difference to push the electric current around the circuit. The light bulb is part of the circuit, and glows brightly when electricity passes through it.

SWITCH

CARBON ROD OF BATTERY

CONTACT BETWEEN SIDE OF BULB AND BRASS STRIP

CONTACT BETWEEN BASE OF BULB AND BATTERY

BULB

REFLECTOR

PROTECTIVE GLASS

△ **Inside a torch**
The electrical circuit inside a torch begins at the batteries. The current flows out of one battery, along the brass strip, through the switch when it is 'on', through the light bulb, and out of the bulb's base, back to the batteries.

Changing current

The switch in a torch opens and closes a gap in the circuit. When the gap is open, the circuit is

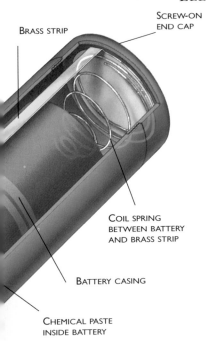

BRASS STRIP

SCREW-ON END CAP

COIL SPRING BETWEEN BATTERY AND BRASS STRIP

BATTERY CASING

CHEMICAL PASTE INSIDE BATTERY

broken. Electricity cannot flow through the air in the gap. When the switch is turned on, the ends of the metal strip touch each other. The gap is closed and electricity can flow.

The device called a thermocouple produces small amounts of electricity simply from the temperature difference between two places (see below). Thermocouples are used as thermometers for measuring temperatures very accurately.

▽ *Making electricity with temperature*
A thermocouple is a circuit with two wires of different metals, such as copper and iron. The places where the wires join are called junctions. If the junctions are at the same temperature, no electricity flows. A temperature difference between the junctions makes electricity flow.

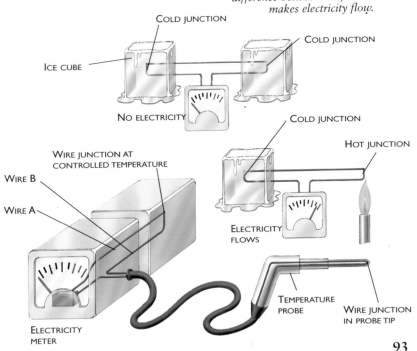

COLD JUNCTION

COLD JUNCTION

ICE CUBE

NO ELECTRICITY

WIRE JUNCTION AT CONTROLLED TEMPERATURE

WIRE B

WIRE A

COLD JUNCTION

HOT JUNCTION

ELECTRICITY FLOWS

ELECTRICITY METER

TEMPERATURE PROBE

WIRE JUNCTION IN PROBE TIP

ELECTRICITY SUPPLY

All electrical gadgets and machines need a supply of electricity to keep them working. The usual sources are the mains supply from wall sockets, and batteries of many shapes and sizes. A battery contains energy in the form of chemicals, which is changed to electrical energy when the battery is connected into a circuit.

Many electrical devices, such as light bulbs, computers and washing machines, use mains electricity. Some of them plug into sockets in the wall. Behind the sockets and lights, safely hidden in the walls and ceilings, are mains wires. These are connected to a distribution board or 'fuse box', which is where the electricity comes into the house along a mains supply cable under the ground.

The mains supply cable goes to other houses and buildings, too. In some places it is above the ground, on poles, rather than being buried underground.

The electricity in the mains supply cable comes from an electricity generating station, or power station. This could be many kilometres away. The huge

▽ **Hydroelectricity**
A hydroelectric dam holds water back, behind it. The water flows through turbines in the dam which spin electricity generators (see page 78).

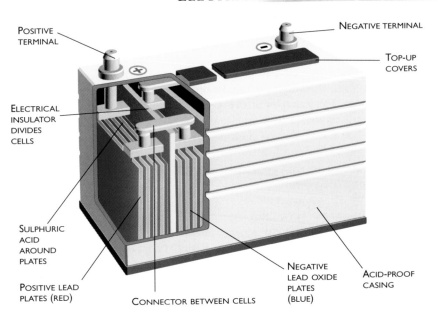

POSITIVE TERMINAL

NEGATIVE TERMINAL

TOP-UP COVERS

ELECTRICAL INSULATOR DIVIDES CELLS

SULPHURIC ACID AROUND PLATES

POSITIVE LEAD PLATES (RED)

CONNECTOR BETWEEN CELLS

NEGATIVE LEAD OXIDE PLATES (BLUE)

ACID-PROOF CASING

△ **Stored electricity**
A vehicle's storage battery, or accumulator, contains metal plates and acid chemicals. When connected into a circuit, these substances react together to produce electricity, which starts the vehicle. As the vehicle goes along, its engine provides power to recharge the battery.

cables from the power station are usually high above the ground, on tall pylons. They bring very powerful high-voltage electricity, tens of thousands of volts, to local sub-stations. Here the electricity is made less powerful, by transformers, so that it is 220 or 110 volts, suited for ordinary houses.

Battery power

Batteries hold electrical energy in chemical form. They power portable electrical machines, such as torches, radios, toys, CD players, mobile telephones and laptop computers.

Inside a battery are chemicals which react together to release electrons. As the battery is used up, this means the chemicals inside it are gradually being used up. Some batteries, such as car batteries, can be recharged by sending electricity back into them.

FACTS ABOUT ELECTRICITY

▶ The strength or pushing force of electricity is measured in volts. UK mains electricity is 220-240 volts. A torch battery is about 1.5 or 3 volts.

▶ The amount or quantity of electricity is measured in amps.

▶ The power of electricity, which is the rate at which electrical energy is used, is measured in watts. A normal light bulb is 60 or 100 watts.

MAGNETISM

Magnets are very useful – and more widespread than many people think. You may have magnets for sticking notes to the fridge, magnets in door latches to keep them closed, and perhaps a magnetic desk-tidy for paper clips and pins.

COMPASS LINES UP WITH
EARTH'S NATURAL LINES
OF MAGNETIC FORCE

There are also magnets hidden away inside almost every electrical machine. For example, each electric motor has a magnet.

A magnetic material is a substance which can be turned into a magnet. This means it attracts other magnetic materials. But only a very few materials are magnetic. The most common one is the metal iron. Since iron is the main substance in steel, then steel is magnetic, too. Many household items, from pins and cutlery to kitchen utensils and tools, are made of steel (see page 30).

▽ *Magnetic fields*
A compass needle is a small needle-shaped magnet than can pivot freely. Its red end tends to be attracted to the Earth's natural Magnetic North Pole (above). But a bar magnet brought nearby overpowers the Earth's weak magnetism. So the compass aligns with the bar magnet instead (below).

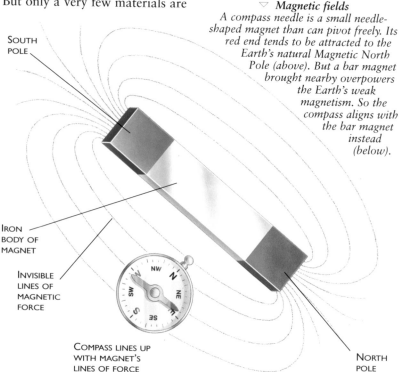

SOUTH
POLE

IRON
BODY OF
MAGNET

INVISIBLE
LINES OF
MAGNETIC
FORCE

COMPASS LINES UP
WITH MAGNET'S
LINES OF FORCE

NORTH
POLE

Types of magnet

The sort of magnet you stick to your fridge door is called a permanent magnet, because it always works as a magnet. Other objects can be temporary magnets. For example, if you pick up a steel paper clip with a permanent magnet, then the paper clip temporarily becomes a magnet itself. It can pick up another paper clip, and so on. When the permanent magnet is taken away, the paper clip stops being a magnet. The temporary magnetism in the paper clip is called induced magnetism.

Magnetic fields

All magnets have a space around them where their magnetism can be felt. This is called a magnetic field. The field is always strongest

FACTS ABOUT MAGNETS

▶ The normal type of magnetism, where iron-containing substances become magnetized, is known as ferromagnetism.

▶ The type of rock called magnetite is naturally magnetic, when dug from the ground. Thin slivers of it were used for the first magnetic compasses. Some types of magnetite are also known as lodestone.

▶ The strength or power of a magnetic field is measured in units called teslas.

at two places on the magnet, which are called magnetic poles. One pole is called the north pole and the other is the south pole. If you put two magnets next to each other, then opposite or unlike poles – north and south – attract each other. Like poles, such as two north poles, or two south ones, repel or push away from each other.

Magnetic Earth

Planet Earth works like a giant magnet. It has a magnetic field, which we can detect with a small magnetized needle, called a compass. The magnetic poles of the Earth are known as the Magnetic North Pole and Magnetic South Pole. They are near, but not quite at the same place as, the real or Geographic North and South Poles (see page 104).

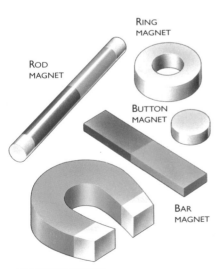

RING MAGNET

ROD MAGNET

BUTTON MAGNET

BAR MAGNET

HORSESHOE MAGNET

◁ *Different shapes of magnets*
Some permanent magnets are shaped like bars or horseshoes. But they can also be made like buttons or discs.

ELECTROMAGNETISM

Whenever an electric current flows through a wire, the wire acts like a magnet, and a magnetic field forms round it. The magnetism caused by electricity is called electromagnetism. The magnets made in this way are known as electromagnets. They are useful because their magnetism can be turned on and off, by turning the electric current in them on and off.

An electric current flowing along a straight wire creates a magnetic field around the wire. But the magnetism is very weak. However, if the wire is wrapped round and round, as a coil, it makes a much stronger magnetic field when electricity flows through it. A piece of iron, called a core, in the middle of the coil makes it stronger still.

Most electromagnets have this design, with a coil of wire – often many thousands of turns – around a bar-shaped iron core. The coil of wire itself is known as a solenoid.

Using electromagnets

One common use for electromagnets is in automatic door latches. When the electromagnet inside the latch is turned on, it attracts a lump of iron which is attached to the bolt in the latch. This slides the bolt sideways, to unlock the door.

▽ *The electric car*
A modern car contains many small electromagnets and electric motors. They work the centrally-operated door locks, the windscreen wipers, the window-moving motors, the petrol pump and many other mechanisms.

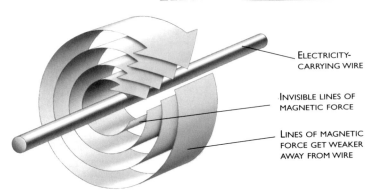

ELECTRICITY-CARRYING WIRE

INVISIBLE LINES OF MAGNETIC FORCE

LINES OF MAGNETIC FORCE GET WEAKER AWAY FROM WIRE

▷ **Electric magnetism**
When electricity passes through a wire, it creates a weak magnetic field around the wire (above). Wrapping the wire into a coil shape around an iron bar, or core, makes the magnetism much stronger (right). This is an electromagnet.

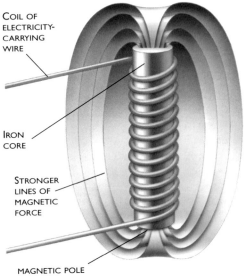

COIL OF ELECTRICITY-CARRYING WIRE

IRON CORE

STRONGER LINES OF MAGNETIC FORCE

MAGNETIC POLE

Electromagnets also make sound in loudspeakers (see page 61). Varying electrical signals passing through the electromagnetic coil alternately attract and repel a permanent magnet attached to the loudspeaker cone. The changing current makes the cone vibrate backwards and forwards, which produces sounds.

Electric motors

Inside a simple electric motor there is a coil of wire, called an armature, which spins on a central shaft. The armature is surrounded by permanent magnets. When a current flows through the coil, the coil becomes an electromagnet. Its magnetic poles are attracted to the unlike poles of the permanent magnets. This makes the armature turn around until the poles line up. But then a switch system reverses the current in the coil. This reverses its magnetic poles – which makes the coil turn again, and so on. The process is repeated many times each second, making the armature spin around.

ELECTRONIC COMMUNICATIONS

When you make a telephone call, watch television, listen to the radio, send a fax or an e-mail, or hook up your computer to the Internet, you are making use of electronic communications. Information is sent using electronic devices and circuits, coded as patterns of electrical signals, laser light pulses, radio waves or microwaves.

▷ *Radio waves*
Invisible radio waves are one of the many kinds of electro-magnetic waves. They are sent out, or broadcast, from antennae (aerials) on tall towers. They carry radio and television programmes, mobile phone calls and many other forms of communication.

When you talk into a telephone, a tiny microphone in the mouthpiece changes the sounds of your voice into patterns of electrical signals. These signals travel through the wires and cables of the telecommunications network to the telephone of the person you are talking to. There, they are changed back into sounds by a small loudspeaker in the telephone earpiece.

Telecommunications means communication – passing information and knowledge – over long distances. The detailed workings of the telecom network are enormously complicated and rely on thousands of different types of electronic machines and devices. Sometimes the coded signals travel in electrical

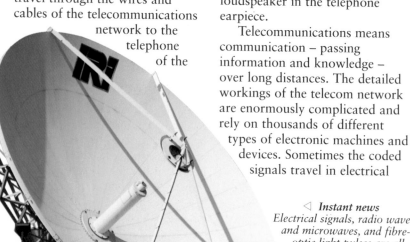

◁ *Instant news*
Electrical signals, radio waves and microwaves, and fibre-optic light pulses are all electromagnetic waves. So they all travel at the speed of light. They can pass around the Earth in only one-seventh of a second, via huge dish-shaped antennae.

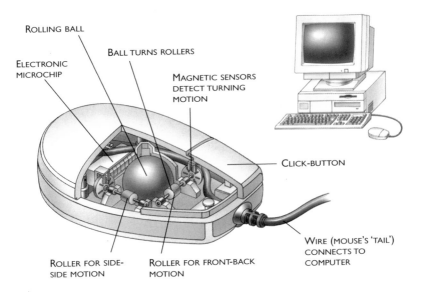

ROLLING BALL

BALL TURNS ROLLERS

ELECTRONIC MICROCHIP

MAGNETIC SENSORS DETECT TURNING MOTION

CLICK-BUTTON

WIRE (MOUSE'S 'TAIL') CONNECTS TO COMPUTER

ROLLER FOR SIDE-SIDE MOTION

ROLLER FOR FRONT-BACK MOTION

△ **The essential computer**
A computer is a vital piece of equipment for many forms of telecommunications. Its mouse is a simple electronic device that moves the cursor on the screen, with a button to make or select choices from lists or menus.

form along wires, all the way. But for longer journeys, they may be changed into invisible radio waves that pass through the air. Walkie-talkie radios and mobile telephones also use radio waves.

Any form of information can be turned into patterns of coded signals. This includes the sounds of a telephone call, pictures and words on a computer or television screen, and various forms of computer data.

Comsats

In other sections of the telecom system, signals are sent as coded patterns of microwaves. Radio waves or microwaves may beam up to a comsat (communications satellite) in space. This strengthens or amplifies them and sends them back down to a receiving station thousands of kilometres away.

Fibre-optics

In some parts of the network, the signals become pulses of laser light that travel along fibre-optic cables. A fibre-optic cable is a bundle of flexible glass rods, each thinner than a hair, but incredibly long. The flashes of light bounce in a zig-zag way along the inside of the rod. A fibre-optic cable the thickness of a finger contains thousands of rods and can carry millions of telephone calls or dozens of cable television channels.

EARTH AND SPACE

We are used to seeing things on a human scale. So tall trees, cliffs and skyscrapers seem large to us. Even from the top of a high hill, we can only see a few dozen kilometres in each direction. So it is very difficult for us to imagine the enormous size of our planet, Earth. It is even more difficult to imagine that the Earth is just a tiny speck, in one tiny corner, in one tiny part of the Universe.

To most people, the surface of the Earth seems still and solid. But if you live near a volcano, or in an area where earthquakes happen, you would know that our globe is far from unchanging.

The solid part of the Earth that we stand on is called the crust. The whole Earth is more than 12,000 kilometres across. But the crust is only about 30-40 kilometres thick under the land,

and 5-10 kilometres thick under the oceans. Compared to the size of the whole planet, the crust is thinner, in proportion, than the skin on an apple.

Underneath the crust is a layer of hot, semi-melted rocks called the mantle. Under the mantle is the Earth's core, which is even hotter, more than 6,000°C. It contains huge amounts of the metals iron and nickel.

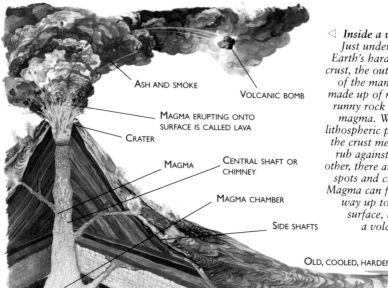

ASH AND SMOKE

VOLCANIC BOMB

MAGMA ERUPTING ONTO SURFACE IS CALLED LAVA

CRATER

MAGMA

CENTRAL SHAFT OR CHIMNEY

MAGMA CHAMBER

SIDE SHAFTS

OLD, COOLED, HARDENED LAVA

◁ *Inside a volcano*
Just under the Earth's hard outer crust, the outer layer of the mantle is made up of molten, runny rock called magma. Where lithospheric plates in the crust meet and rub against each other, there are weak spots and cracks. Magma can force its way up to the surface, creating a volcano.

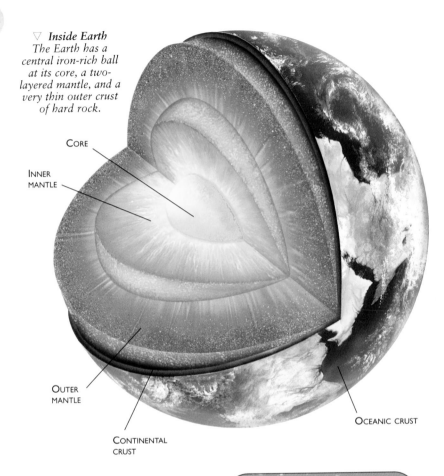

▽ *Inside Earth*
The Earth has a central iron-rich ball at its core, a two-layered mantle, and a very thin outer crust of hard rock.

CORE

INNER MANTLE

OUTER MANTLE

CONTINENTAL CRUST

OCEANIC CRUST

Plates and 'quakes

The Earth's crust is not all one piece, like the shell on a coconut. It has cracks in it which divide it into huge curved pieces called lithospheric plates. These are moving about slowly. In some places they are drifting apart, leaving huge slits and valleys. In others they are pushing together and crumpling, to cause earthquakes and form mountains.

FACTS ABOUT EARTH

▸ The Earth is not quite a perfect ball-shaped sphere. It is slightly wider at the line around its middle or widest part, the Equator, and slightly flattened at the top and bottom, the Poles.

▸ The average distance from the centre of the Earth to its surface (that is, the radius of the Earth) is 6,375 kilometres.

▸ The distance around the Equator is about 40,000 kilometres.

DAYLIGHT AND DARKNESS

The Earth spins around an imaginary line which goes from the Geographic North Pole, through the centre of the planet to the Geographic South Pole. This line is called the Earth's axis. The Earth turns around it once every 24 hours. Since the Sun shines at the Earth from the side, half the Earth is in daylight and the other half is in darkness.

△ *Sun-powered Earth*
The Sun's light allows us and other animals to see and move about safely. It also provides energy for plants to live and grow. Plants feed animals, and so animals depend on the Sun for food.

▽ *The changing Moon*
The Moon shines because it reflects sunlight. As the Earth spins on its axis, the Moon – like the Sun – seems to move across the sky. And as the Moon goes around or orbits the Earth, its sunlit side changes when seen from Earth. We call these changes the phases of the Moon.

The Sun seems to move across the sky each day. But really, it is the Earth that is moving. When a place on the Earth is on the side lit by the Sun, it has daytime. As the Earth spins, this place moves around. The Sun seems to sink below the horizon at dusk. The place moves around to the far side, away from the Sun. Then it is dark, and night-time. The Earth continues to spin, the Sun seems to come up over the horizon at dawn, and it is daytime again.

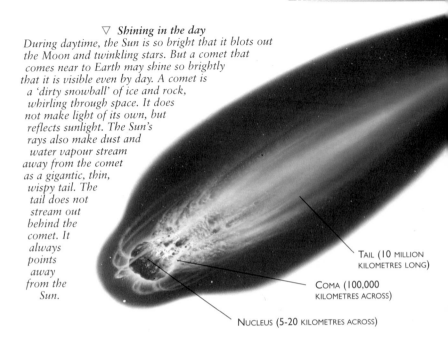

▽ **Shining in the day**
During daytime, the Sun is so bright that it blots out the Moon and twinkling stars. But a comet that comes near to Earth may shine so brightly that it is visible even by day. A comet is a 'dirty snowball' of ice and rock, whirling through space. It does not make light of its own, but reflects sunlight. The Sun's rays also make dust and water vapour stream away from the comet as a gigantic, thin, wispy tail. The tail does not stream out behind the comet. It always points away from the Sun.

TAIL (10 MILLION KILOMETRES LONG)

COMA (100,000 KILOMETRES ACROSS)

NUCLEUS (5-20 KILOMETRES ACROSS)

The seasons

The seasons are caused by the movement of the Earth around the Sun. The Earth's axis is not upright, but tilted slightly on its side. So for half the year, the upper or northern part of the Earth is tilted nearer the Sun. It is warmer in the north. We call it summer. The southern half of the Earth is tilted farther away from the Sun, and it is cooler – winter. For the other half of the year, the southern part of the Earth is nearer the Sun and has summer, while the north has its winter.

EXPLORING SPACE

The Earth's pull of gravity is so strong that only a rocket engine is powerful enough to escape it. Rockets launch many kinds of spacecraft, such as Earth-orbiting satellites, manned space stations and deep-space probes.

More than three thousand man-made satellites are going around, or orbiting, the Earth. Some are comsats, for communications. They relay or

△ **Shuttle blast-off**
The US Space Shuttle goes into space and comes back to Earth for re-use.

▽ **Landing on the Moon**
Six manned Apollo craft landed on the Moon between 1969 and 1972.

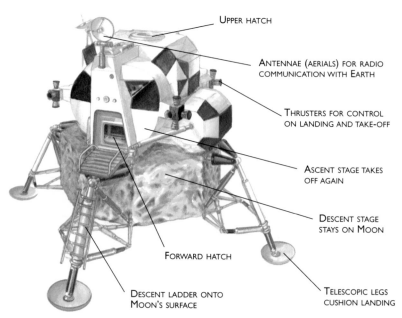

UPPER HATCH

ANTENNAE (AERIALS) FOR RADIO COMMUNICATION WITH EARTH

THRUSTERS FOR CONTROL ON LANDING AND TAKE-OFF

ASCENT STAGE TAKES OFF AGAIN

DESCENT STAGE STAYS ON MOON

FORWARD HATCH

DESCENT LADDER ONTO MOON'S SURFACE

TELESCOPIC LEGS CUSHION LANDING

send on telephone calls, radio messages and television pictures around the Earth. Weather satellites take photographs and measurements of clouds and other weather features, and beam these to Earth for forecasters. Research satellites detect features such as the heat coming from different parts of the Earth, or ozone in different parts of the atmosphere. Spy satellites keep track of ships, planes, tanks and other military equipment.

Space probes

Spacecraft which travel far away from Earth, to the Sun, other planets and beyond, are called space probes. They have cameras to take photographs, and sensors which record other information, such as temperature, the presence of dust and other particles, and the strength of various rays. Some probes fly past other planets. Others go into orbit around them, or even land on the surface.

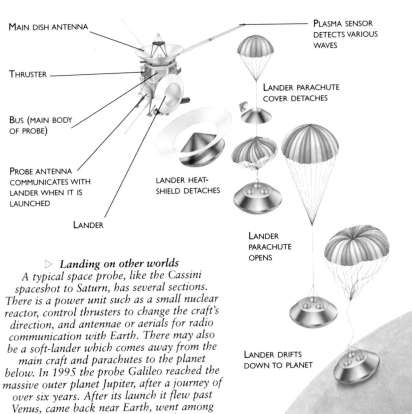

MAIN DISH ANTENNA

PLASMA SENSOR DETECTS VARIOUS WAVES

THRUSTER

LANDER PARACHUTE COVER DETACHES

BUS (MAIN BODY OF PROBE)

PROBE ANTENNA COMMUNICATES WITH LANDER WHEN IT IS LAUNCHED

LANDER HEAT-SHIELD DETACHES

LANDER

LANDER PARACHUTE OPENS

LANDER DRIFTS DOWN TO PLANET

▷ *Landing on other worlds*
A typical space probe, like the Cassini spaceshot to Saturn, has several sections. There is a power unit such as a small nuclear reactor, control thrusters to change the craft's direction, and antennae or aerials for radio communication with Earth. There may also be a soft-lander which comes away from the main craft and parachutes to the planet below. In 1995 the probe Galileo reached the massive outer planet Jupiter, after a journey of over six years. After its launch it flew past Venus, came back near Earth, went among the asteroids, and came near Earth again, before heading out to Jupiter and its moons.

THE SUN

At night, we can see tiny stars twinkling in the endless blackness of space. By day, we can see a star, too – but only one. It is so near to us that it is like a gigantic glowing ball of flames, providing heat and light for our world. This star is the Sun. (The Sun is so bright that it can damage our eyes. Never, ever, look directly at the Sun.)

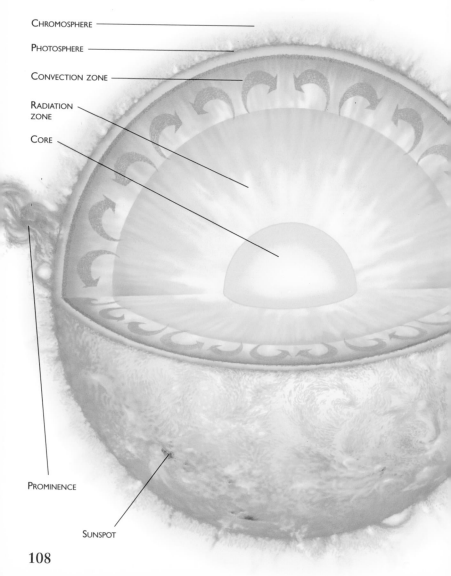

CHROMOSPHERE

PHOTOSPHERE

CONVECTION ZONE

RADIATION ZONE

CORE

PROMINENCE

SUNSPOT

◁ *Inside the Sun*
The Sun is more than nine-tenths hydrogen, along with some helium, and tiny amounts of other substances. It produces its gigantic amounts of energy by nuclear fusion in its very dense central part, the core. The energy is carried outwards through the radiation zone. Then it swirls around, up and down in the next layer, the convection zone, which is about 150,000 kilometres deep. It finally leaves the Sun as light, heat and other waves through its main outer layer, the photosphere. This is the yellow glowing surface that we see from Earth.

The Sun is a fairly small, typical star. It sends out, or radiates, immense amounts of energy. This energy includes light, heat and other types of electromagnetic waves. The Sun also gives off atomic particles of various kinds, which form the solar wind.

How the Sun shines

The energy that the Sun sends out into space comes from nuclear fusion inside the Sun. The central parts, or nuclei, from atoms of the gas hydrogen in the Sun join together, or fuse. They form different atoms, of the gas helium. During the change from hydrogen to helium, tiny amounts of matter are converted into incredible amounts of energy.

The Sun has been burning like this for about 5,000 million years. It will probably go on shining in the same way, as an immense glowing ball of gas, for a similar amount of time. Then it may begin to fade (see page 112).

Probing the Sun

Several space probes have travelled near to the Sun, to measure its temperature and other features. The information is sent back to Earth in the form of coded patterns of radio waves. The Sun is so far away that its light rays, and radio waves from nearby probes, take more than eight minutes to get back to Earth.

The Sun, like the Earth, has its own magnetic field. This magnetism becomes strengthened and concentrated into darker areas on the Sun's surface, known as sunspots. About every 11 years, there is an increase in the number and activity of sunspots. This affects the weather on Earth, causing storms and interference with radio and television.

FACTS ABOUT THE SUN

▸ The Sun is 1,392,000 kilometres across. More than one million Earths would fit inside it.

▸ Like the planets, the Sun spins around on its axis. It turns once about every 25 days and 9 hours.

▸ The average temperature at the Sun's surface is 6,000°C.

▸ The temperature at the Sun's centre is probably about 15,000,000 (15 million) °C.

THE PLANETS

The Earth is just one of a group of planets which orbit the Sun. There are eight others. Each is different in size, shape, structure and surface features. Some of the other planets have smaller objects, moons, going around them. Together the Sun, the planets and their moons make up the Solar System.

The innermost four planets are Mercury, Venus, Earth and Mars. They are relatively small and made mainly of rock. Then there is a huge gap, where small bits of dust and rocks orbit the Sun. These are known as asteroids.

Beyond the asteroids are the next four planets. These are Jupiter, Saturn, Uranus and Neptune. They are huge and made mainly of gases, so they are known as 'gas giants'.

Farthest from the Sun, and the smallest planet of all, is Pluto. Like Earth, Pluto has one moon. It is called Charon, and it is almost half as big across as Pluto itself.

△ *Mercury, nearest the Sun*
Mercury is very hot, because it is so near the Sun. On the side facing the Sun, the temperature soars to more than 450°C, hot enough to set fire to many substances on Earth. But the other, night-time side is minus 180°C.

Days and years

The farther a planet is from the Sun, the longer it takes to complete one journey around the Sun, called an orbit. The time taken for one orbit is the planet's year. We are used to our own year, on Earth, which lasts 365 days. Mercury goes around the Sun in much less time, just 88 Earth days. Pluto takes far longer. Its year lasts 248 Earth years.

Like Earth, all the planets also spin on their axes. The time for one spin around is the length of the planet's day. On Earth, it is 24 hours. The giant planet Jupiter spins so fast that its day lasts just 10 Earth hours. On Venus, a day lasts 243 Earth days – 8 days longer than Venus' year!

◁ *Mars, the red planet*
Through a telescope, Mars looks reddish-yellow because of its surface dust and rocks. Space probes have visited the planet, but found no life.

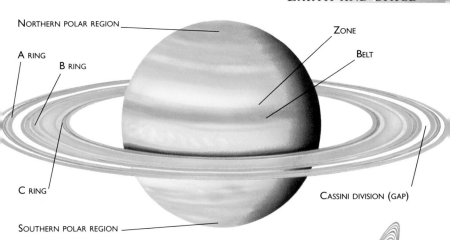

NORTHERN POLAR REGION

A RING

B RING

ZONE

BELT

C RING

SOUTHERN POLAR REGION

CASSINI DIVISION (GAP)

△ *Saturn, planet of rings*
Several planets have rings. These are thin,
circular, shining layers of dust, small rocks and
ice crystals, captured by the planet's gravity.
The most noticeable and spectacular are the
rings of Saturn. The planet itself has striped
areas know as belts, separated by lighter areas,
zones. These are variations in the density and
temperature of its gases.

▷ *Uranus, planet on its side*
All the planets spin in the same direction, anti-
clockwise when seen from above. Except for
Venus and Uranus, which turn the opposite way.
Also most of the planets spin in a fairly upright
position when seen from the side. But Uranus
spins and lies on its side.

FACTS ABOUT THE PLANETS

PLANET	DISTANCE FROM SUN (millions of kilometres)	DIAMETER (thousands of kilometres)	LENGTH OF DAY (Earth hours or days)	LENGTH OF YEAR (Earth days or years)
Mercury	58	4,880	58.6 days	88 days
Venus	108	12,104	243 days	224.7 days
Earth	149.6	12,756	24 hours	365.3 days
Mars	228	6,787	25 hours	687 days
Jupiter	778	143,000	10 hours	11.9 years
Saturn	1,427	120,000	10 hours	29.5 years
Uranus	2,875	51,100	23 hours	84 years
Neptune	4,497	49,500	16 hours	165 years
Pluto	5,900	2,200	6 days	248 years

111

DEEP SPACE

The Sun, planets and moons of our Solar System seem gigantic beyond belief. Yet the Solar System is just a tiny speck in the vastness of the entire Universe.

The night sky glitters with thousands of specks of light. Most are stars, like our Sun. They look so small because they are so far away. Look through binoculars, and you see thousands more stars. A telescope shows yet thousands more.

Some of these stars are hundreds of times larger and brighter than our Sun. Some are smaller and dimmer. All the stars that we can see in the night sky are in a huge cloud of stars called the Milky Way.

Galaxies

The Milky Way is a gathering or clump of stars, called a galaxy. It contains hundreds of millions of stars. This may seem a lot. But the Milky Way is only one galaxy among millions in the Universe.

There are many other objects in deep space. Quasars glow with the energy of a thousand galaxies, yet are only the size of our Solar System. Modern science cannot yet explain them. There is still much to be learned about space.

▽ *The life of a star*
Stars are born, grow and change over billions of years. They begin as faint clouds of gas and dust, called nebulae, drifting in space. The gas and dust clump together into a young star, which begins to glow. Some smaller stars gradually get bigger and shine more brightly, as red giants, then fade away into tiny, planet-sized white dwarfs. Bigger stars swell to supergiant size and then explode as an immense ball of blinding energy, a supernova. The remains shrink under their own gravity into a neutron star, or perhaps a black hole.

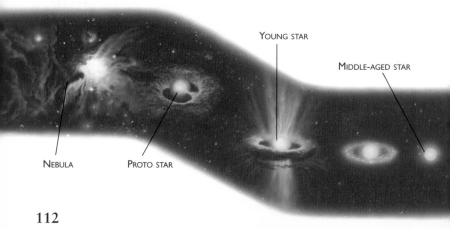

YOUNG STAR

MIDDLE-AGED STAR

NEBULA   PROTO STAR

△ *The final frontier*
Light takes at least 100,000 years to travel across an average galaxy like our own Milky Way. The speed of light is the fastest possible speed, according to modern science. So, even if a spaceship could travel at only a tiny fraction of the speed of light, it would take hundreds or thousands of years to reach faraway stars and planets in other galaxies. For the present, intergalactic travel is still very definitely limited to the stories and movies of science fiction.

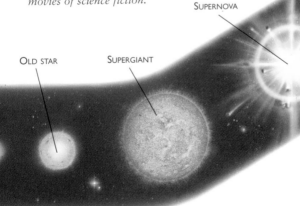

WHITE DWARF

SUPERNOVA

OLD STAR

SUPERGIANT

BLACK HOLE

CHEMICAL ELEMENTS

O ne of the basic sets of information in all of science is the list of chemical substances, called elements (see page 22). The list can be drawn as a large chart known as the periodic table of chemical elements. There are about 112 elements so far discovered. Of these, about 90 are natural, occurring on and in planet Earth, or among the planets and stars in space. The rest have been made, or synthesized, in chemistry and physics laboratories.

All matter in the Universe is composed of the basic substances known as chemical elements. The periodic table, shown on the right, groups the elements according to their similarities and differences. These are physical, both in the way their atoms are made up of smaller particles, and in the physical features of an element, such as its weight and density. They are also chemical, in the way that the element reacts or combines chemically with other

H hydrogen 1						
Li lithium 3	Be beryllium 4					
Na sodium 11	Mg magnesium 12					
K potassium 19	Ca calcium 20	Sc scandium 21	Ti titanium 22	V vanadium 23	Cr chromium 24	Mn manganese 25
Rb rubidium 37	Sr strontium 38	Y yttrium 39	Zr zirconium 40	Nb niobium 41	Mo molybdenum 42	Tc technetium 43
Cs caesium 55	Ba barium 56	Lu lutetium 71	Hf hafnium 72	Ta tantalum 73	W tungsten 74	Re rhenium 75
Fr francium 87	Ra radium 88	Lr lawrencium 103	Rf rutherfordium 104	Db dubnium 105	Sg seaborgium 106	Bh bohrium 107

ALKALI METALS

| La lanthanum 57 | Ce cerium 58 | Pr praseodymium 59 | Nd neodymium 60 | Pm promethium 61 |
| Ac actinium 89 | Th thorium 90 | Pa protactinium 91 | U uranium 92 | Np neptunium 93 |

△ **Most common element**
Hydrogen is the most common element in the Universe. It forms the bulk of each star, and there are billions of stars.

substances (see page 23).
Each element has its own name, such as carbon, iron, aluminium, boron, lithium or zinc. Some names are taken from ancient Latin, Greek or other languages. Other elements are named after their discoverers or generally famous scientists. Arsenic, a very poisonous element, gets its name from *arsenikon*, the old Greek name for the yellow mineral 'orpiment', which is rich in arsenic.

The chemical symbol for each element is one or two letters, usually taken from a shortened version of the full name. It is an international symbol, recognized by scientists all over the world.

The atomic number of an element is the number of the particles called protons inside the nucleus of each atom of the element. This number of protons is the same as the number of electrons whizzing around the nucleus of the atom.

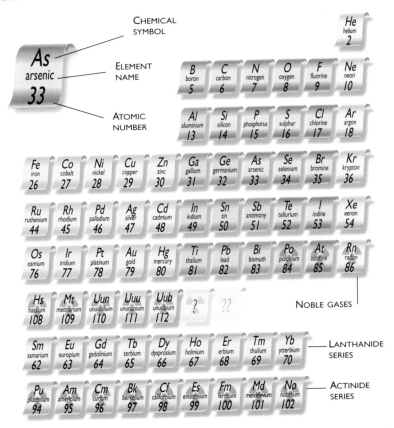

115

REACTIVE METALS AND RARE EARTHS

In the periodic table (see page 114), the elements in the far left column are called the alkali metals. They combine or react very readily with other elements.

| H |
| hydrogen |
| 1 |

The table of elements is known as the periodic table because the chemical features of the elements in each column, one below the other, are similar. They occur with a periodicity – that is, in a regular cycle.

| Li |
| lithium |
| 3 |

For example, the elements in the far left column include lithium, sodium, potassium, rubidium and caesium. These are all metallic elements, and they are all very reactive. This

| Na |
| sodium |
| 11 |

| K |
| potassium |
| 19 |

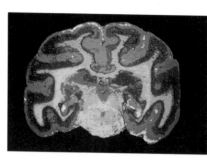

△ **Sodium in the brain**
The millions of nerve signals flashing around the brain have a chemical basis. They are made by sodium and potassium moving into and out of nerve cells.

means they join or react easily with other substances. So in nature they are rarely found on their own, in pure element form.

This first column of elements is called the alkali metals. This is because they react with other substances to form alkalis, which are the opposite of acids. Sodium joins with oxygen and hydrogen

| Rb |
| rubidium |
| 37 |

| Cs |
| caesium |
| 55 |

La	Ce	Pr	Nd	Pm	Sm
lanthanum	cerium	praseodymium	neodymium	promethium	samarium
57	58	59	60	61	62

Ac	Th	Pa	U	Np	Pu
actinium	thorium	protactinium	uranium	neptunium	plutonium
89	90	91	92	93	94

| Fr |
| francium |
| 87 |

◁ **Useful, but not as metals**
Alkali metals are useful when combined with other substances, but not as pure metals. They combine with air and burst into flames!

to form sodium hydroxide, NaOH. This is better known as caustic soda. It is a powerful alkali that can burn skin. It is used as a drain-cleaner and in the manufacture of paper, artificial fibres, soaps and detergents.

Rare earth elements

The two sets of elements shown below do not quite fit into the main periodic table. They are known as the lanthanide series and the actinide series, after the first element in each group. They are also called 'rare earths' because the lanthanides occur only rarely in the rocks of the Earth.

All the elements in the lanthanide series are very similar to each other. They are also similar to a more familiar element, the shiny metal called aluminium.

The elements in the actinide series are also similar to the lanthanides and to each other. But they are synthetic elements – they have been created in science laboratories.

> FACTS ABOUT ALKALI METALS
> ▶ Many alkali metals and other metals are used in alloys. An alloy is a mixture or a compound of two or more metals, or of a metal and a non-metal.
> ▶ Lithium is used in some very lightweight alloys of aluminium or magnesium. It is also used in certain medical drugs for mental conditions such as severe depression.
> ▶ Rubidium is used in tiny amounts in photo-electric or 'solar' cells, which generate electricity when light shines on them. It also works as a 'getter' for combining with and removing impurities in chemical processes.
> ▶ Caesium is also used in photo-electric cells

▽ *Lanthanides and actinides*
These two rows or series of elements are shown below left and below (and in the full periodic table on pages 114-115). They are also known as the rare earth metals.

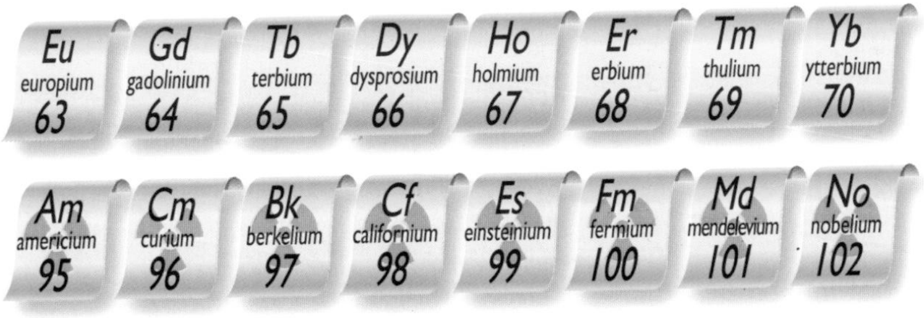

Eu europium 63	Gd gadolinium 64	Tb terbium 65	Dy dysprosium 66	Ho holmium 67	Er erbium 68	Tm thulium 69	Yb ytterbium 70

Am americium 95	Cm curium 96	Bk berkelium 97	Cf californium 98	Es einsteinium 99	Fm fermium 100	Md mendelevium 101	No nobelium 102

△ *Americium*
This element was made in 1945 by bombarding a form of uranium.

△ *Radioactivity*
All actinide elements are radioactive, as shown by the orange symbol.

METALS AND MORE METALS

Most elements are metals. This means they are generally hard and shiny, tough and strong, and they conduct or carry electricity and heat well. They have thousands of uses in daily life, often mixed or combined with each other to form alloys.

△ **Many kinds of metals**
An enormously complex machine like the Space Shuttle contains hundreds of different alloys.

Almost any machine or device has at least one metal in it. Iron is one of the most widely-used metals. It is combined with small amounts of the non-metal carbon, to form the group of alloys known as steels.

There are hundreds of kinds of steels. Each one has been carefully developed to have different qualities of hardness, stiffness, lightness, resistance to corrosion and other features. In most steels, the proportion of carbon is less than one-twentieth.

Iron makes steel

Steel plate forms the large sheets in washing machines, cars, trains and ships. The stainless steel used for making cutlery and cooking utensils is an alloy with at least one-tenth of the extremely hard, shiny metal known as chromium. Steels with titanium in them form the light but stiff structural sheets in high-speed aircraft.

Sc scandium 21	Ti titanium 22	V vanadium 23	Cr chromium 24
Y yttrium 39	Zr zirconium 40	Nb niobium 41	Mo molybdenum 42
Lu lutetium 71	Hf hafnium 72	Ta tantalum 73	W tungsten 74
Lr lawrencium 103	Rf rutherfordium 104	Db dubnium 105	Sg seaborgium 106

| La lanthanum 57 |
| Ac actinium 89 |

△ **Tungsten (W)**
Formerly known as wolfram, this metal has an incredibly high melting point, 3,410°C. This makes it suitable for use in high-speed objects where friction creates enormous heat, such as in jet engines and the tips of high-speed drills.

FACTS ABOUT METALS

▸ Most pure metals are, surprisingly, not that hard or tough. This is why the science of alloys, combining metals with each other or with different non-metal substances, is so important.

▸ One of the earliest alloys was bronze, a mix of copper and tin. It has been in use for thousands of years and was the first widely-used substance for tools, after rocks and stones.

▸ Brass is another common alloy, made from copper and zinc.

▸ Perhaps the most famous metal is gold. It has been valued and cherished since ancient times because it stays bright and shiny, yet is also easy to work with.

▸ Silver is another long-valued metal. It is the best conductor of electricity of any metal, and is also used in jewellery, photographic film and for coins.

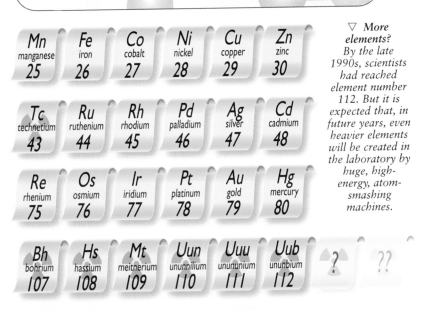

Mn manganese 25	Fe iron 26	Co cobalt 27	Ni nickel 28	Cu copper 29	Zn zinc 30
Tc technetium 43	Ru ruthenium 44	Rh rhodium 45	Pd palladium 46	Ag silver 47	Cd cadmium 48
Re rhenium 75	Os osmium 76	Ir iridium 77	Pt platinum 78	Au gold 79	Hg mercury 80
Bh bohrium 107	Hs hassium 108	Mt meitnerium 109	Uun ununnilium 110	Uuu unununium 111	Uub ununbium 112

▽ **More elements?** By the late 1990s, scientists had reached element number 112. But it is expected that, in future years, even heavier elements will be created in the laboratory by huge, high-energy, atom-smashing machines.

◁ *Developing new alloys* Metallurgists (metal experts) are continually making new combinations and mixtures of metals, to produce better alloys for a range of uses. Steels with chromium and vanadium are exceptionally tough, suited for pipes that must resist wear and corrosion.

119

NON-METALS

There are well over 100 chemical elements. Only about 20 are non-metals. But they include some of the most widespread and important of all elements. For example, oxygen is vital for life, while carbon is the basic element in all living things, and silicon is essential for electronic devices like microchips.

▽ **Combustion**
Burning, or combustion, is when a substance combines with the oxygen in the air, and gives off large amounts of light and heat.

The two most abundant elements on our planet are non-metals. Oxygen accounts for almost one-half of all the substances in the Earth's crust. Silicon accounts for about one-quarter.

Oxygen makes up one-fifth of the air we breathe. It combines with hydrogen to form water (H_2O). It is also found in all kinds of rocks, combined in the form of oxides.

Silicon is also found in combined forms in most kinds of rocks, as oxides such as silica. Ordinary sand on the beach is almost pure silica, SiO_2.

Carbon is another vital non-metal. It forms long chains of atoms linked together, –C–C–C– This feature has allowed it to form the 'backbones' of the molecules in living things. Carbon is so important, and joins with so many other elements, in so many different ways, that it has its own branch of science. This is called organic chemistry.

NON-METALS SHOWN AS MAUVE AND GREY

					He helium 2
B boron 5	C carbon 6	N nitrogen 7	O oxygen 8	F fluorine 9	Ne neon 10
Al aluminium 13	Si silicon 14	P phosphorus 15	S sulphur 16	Cl chlorine 17	Ar argon 18
Ga gallium 31	Ge germanium 32	As arsenic 33	Se selenium 34	Br bromine 35	Kr krypton 36
In indium 49	Sn tin 50	Sb antimony 51	Te tellurium 52	I iodine 53	Xe xenon 54
Ti thalium 81	Pb lead 82	Bi bismuth 83	Po polonium 84	At astatine 85	Rn radon 86

Noble gases

On the far right of the periodic table is the column of elements known as 'noble gases'. They include helium; neon, argon, krypton, xenon and radon. They are the opposite of the alkali metal elements in the far left of the table, in that they hardly react or join with any other elements. They are known as 'inert'. Most occur in tiny quantities in the air around us.

FACTS ABOUT NOBLE GASES

▸ Helium is the second-lightest element, after hydrogen. It is used in balloons and airships since it does not catch fire, like hydrogen.

▸ Neon is used in red 'neon' lights and in lasers.

▸ Argon is also used in light bulbs and tubes, and as a 'blanket' to prevent metals combining with oxygen during high-temperature welding.

▸ Krypton is another gas used in lighting tubes, and in photographic flash units.

UNITS AND MEASUREMENTS

Science depends on accurate measurements. How long? How fast? Exactly where? A vague guess is no good when a skyscraper is being built, or a satellite is sent into space. The units marked * here are the main ones in the International System (SI) used by scientists all over the world.

Basic Measurements

LENGTH
* metre *symbol* **m**

OTHER LENGTH UNITS
1 inch (in) = 2.54 cm
1 foot (ft) = 12 in = 0.3048 m
1 yard (yd) = 3 ft = 0.9144 m
1 mile = 5280 ft = 1.61 km

MASS
* gram *symbol* **g**

OTHER MASS UNITS
1 ounce (oz) = 28.35 g
1 pound (lb) = 16 oz = 0.45 kg
1 ton (imperial) = 2240 lb =
1016 kg = 1.016 tonnes (metric)

TIME
* second *symbol* **s**

OTHER TIME UNITS
60 s = 1 minute
60 minutes = 1 hour
24 hours = 1 day
365.2422 days = 1 year

TEMPERATURE
* kelvin *symbol* **K**

OTHER TEMPERATURE UNITS
°C = kelvin + 273.15
degrees Fahrenheit (°F) =
9/5 degrees Celsius (°C) + 32

ELECTRIC CURRENT.
* ampere *symbol* **A**

LIGHT INTENSITY
* candela *symbol* **cd**

AMOUNT OF MATTER
* mole *symbol* **mol**
1 mol contains the same number
of atoms as 12 g of carbon-12

Derived Measurements

AREA
* square metres *symbol* **m²**

OTHER AREA UNITS
1 hectare = 1,000 m²
1 square foot = 1 sq ft =
144 sq in
1 square yard = 1 sq yd =
9 sq ft
1 acre = 4,840 sq yd

VOLUME
* cubic centimetre *symbol* **cc**
or **cm³**
* litre *symbol* **l**
* cubic metre *symbol* **m³**

OTHER VOLUME UNITS
1 pint = 1 pt = 0.568 l
1 gallon = 1 gal = 8 pts = 4.55 l

DENSITY (mass per unit volume)
* grams per cubic centimetre
symbol **g/cm³**

SPEED OR VELOCITY
(distance moved with time)
* kilometres per hour
symbol **km/h**

OTHER SPEED UNITS
miles per hour *symbol* **mph**

ACCELERATION
(change in velocity with time)
* metres per second per second
symbol **m/s²**

FORCE OR WEIGHT
(mass times acceleration)
* newtons *symbol* **N** or **kgm/s²**

MOMENTUM
(mass times speed)
* kilograms *x* metres per second
symbol **kgm/s**

PRESSURE
(force per unit area)
* newtons per square metre
symbol **N/m²**

OTHER PRESSURE UNITS
1 mm Hg = 133.32 N/m²
1 atmosphere = 760 mm Hg

ENERGY
(force times distance moved)
* joule *symbol* **J**

POWER
(energy used per second)
* watt *symbol* **W**

INDEX

Acknowledgements

The publishers would like to thank the following illustrators and artists, whose works appear in this book:

Julian Baker
Julie Banyard
Julian Barker
Kuo Kang Chen
Andrew Farmer
Mike Foster/Maltings Partnership
Jeremy Gower
Ron Hayward
Gary Hincks
Rob Jakeway
Roger Kent
Aziz Khan
Janos Marffy
Mel Pickering
Terry Riley
Mike Saunders
Guy Smith/Mainline Design

All other images are from MKP Archives.

Thanks also to Lynne French for editorial assistance and to Jane Parker for the Index.